Devil's Advocates

DEVIL'S ADVOCATES is a series of books devoted to exploring the classics of horror cinema. Contributors to the series come from the fields of teaching, academia, journalism and fiction, but all have one thing in common: a passion for the horror film and a desire to share it with the widest possible audience.

'The admirable Devil's Advocates series is not only essential – and fun – reading for the serious horror fan but should be set texts on any genre course.'
Dr Ian Hunter, Reader in Film Studies, De Montfort University, Leicester

'Devil's Advocates critiques on individual titles... offer bracingly fresh perspectives from passionate writers. The series will perfectly complement the BFI archive volumes.' **Christopher Fowler,** *Independent on Sunday*

'Devil's Advocates has proven itself more than capable of producing impassioned, intelligent analyses of genre cinema... quickly becoming the go-to guys for intelligent, easily digestible film criticism.' **Horror Talk.com**

ALSO AVAILABLE IN THIS SERIES

A Girl Walks Home Alone at Night Farshid Kazemi
Black Sunday Martyn Conterio
The Blair Witch Project Peter Turner
Blood and Black Lace Roberto Curti
The Blood on Satan's Claw David Evans-Powell
The Cabin in the Woods Susanne Kord
Candyman Jon Towlson
Cannibal Holocaust Calum Waddell
Cape Fear Rob Daniel
Carrie Neil Mitchell
The Company of Wolves James Gracey
The Conjuring Kevin J. Wetmore Jr.
The Craft Miranda Corcoran
Creepshow Simon Brown
Cruising Eugenio Ercolani & Marcus Stiglegger
The Curse of Frankenstein Marcus K. Harmes
Daughters of Darkness Kat Ellinger
Dawn of the Dead Jon Towlson
Dead of Night Jez Conolly & David Bates
The Descent James Marriot
The Devils Darren Arnold
Don't Look Now Jessica Gildersleeve
The Evil Dead Lloyd Haynes
The Fly Emma Westwood
Frenzy Ian Cooper
Halloween Murray Leeder
House of Usher Evert Jan van Leeuwen
I Walked With a Zombie Clive Dawson
In the Mouth of Madness Michael Blyth
IT Chapters One and Two Alissa Burger
It Follows Joshua Grimm
Ju-on The Grudge Marisa Hayes
Let the Right One In Anne Billson
M Samm Deighan
Macbeth Rebekah Owens
The Mummy Doris V. Sutherland
Nosferatu Cristina Massaccesi
The Omen Adrian Schober
Peeping Tom Kiri Bloom Walden
Poltergeist Rob McLaughlin
Possession Alison Taylor
Re-Animator Eddie Falvey
Repulsion Jeremy Carr
Saw Benjamin Poole
Scream Steven West
The Shining Laura Mee
Shivers Luke Aspell
The Silence of the Lambs Barry Forshaw
Suspiria Alexandra Heller-Nicholas
The Texas Chain Saw Massacre James Rose
The Thing Jez Conolly
Trouble Every Day Kate Robertson
Twin Peaks: Fire Walk With Me Lindsay Hallam
The Wicker Man Steve A. Wiggins
Witchfinder General Ian Cooper

FORTHCOMING

The Woman in Black Mark Fryers & Marcus K. Harmes

Devil's Advocates

The Vanishing

Christina Brennan

Acknowledgements

I thank John Atkinson for commissioning this project and Ally Lee and Christabel Scaife at Liverpool University Press for their advice and support throughout the writing process. I should also thank Anne Sluizer, Anouk Sluizer, and Sluizer Film Productions. They shared valuable insights from production and were enthusiastic about this project from its early stages to publication. I'm also grateful to Dennis Alink for responding to my queries about his documentary *Sluizer Speaks* (2014) and for putting me in touch with Sluizer Film Productions.

Jan Wich's behind-the-scenes stills from the production were a generous contribution to this book, and their inclusion significantly enhanced the final manuscript. The staff at the British Film Institute Reuben Library offered invaluable assistance across multiple trips to their London archive and played a significant role in locating resources for this project. I am also grateful to the Eye Film Institute in Amsterdam for facilitating access to further images. The anonymous reviewers at Liverpool University Press, with their insightful suggestions for improvement on a penultimate draft of this manuscript, also played a crucial role in shaping the final version.

I am always indebted to my parents, Michael and Geraldine, for their generosity and support. I am lucky to have them, and I owe every success, however minor, to them. My partner, Matthew, offered vital encouragement at every stage and was wise to my many attempts to procrastinate. His realism is always mixed with kindness, and he anchors my life with his good heart, good humour, and good sense.

Writing this book was surprisingly enjoyable and straightforward, largely thanks to the support of all the above. If any praise is due, they share all the credit.

First published in 2025 by
Liverpool University Press
4 Cambridge Street
Liverpool
L69 7ZU

Series design: Nikki Hamlett at Cassels Design
Set by Carnegie Book Production, Lancaster

All rights reserved. No part of this publication may be reproduced in any material form (including photocopying or storing in any medium by electronic means and whether or not transiently or incidentally to some other use of this publication) without the permission of the copyright owner.

British Library Cataloguing-in-Publication Data
A catalogue record for this book is available from the British Library
ISBN hardback: 9781836243526
ISBN paperback: 9781836243533
eISBN: 9781836243663

Contents

Synopsis ... 1

Introduction: *Spoorloos* and International Success ... 5

Chapter One: From Adaptation to Screen ... 19

Chapter Two: Lemorne, the Ordinary Everyman, and Psychological Horror ... 29

Chapter Three: A Portrait of a Serial Killer ... 43

Chapter Four: Grief and the Gothic in *Spoorloos* ... 59

Chapter Five: *Spoorloos* as Post-horror Cinema ... 83

Chapter Six: Adaptations and Transformations ... 105

Afterword: *Spoorloos*' Legacy ... 113

Bibliography ... 117

For Matthew

Figures

Figure 1. Lemorne makes his offer to Rex. (Credit to Anouk Sluizer) 13

Figure 2. George Sluizer and Johanna ter Steege on the *Spoorloos* set. (Credit to Jan Wich) 23

Figure 3. Bernard-Pierre Donnadieu on the *Spoorloos* set. (Credit to Jan Wich) 25

Figure 4. George Sluizer and the cast of Lemorne's family. (Credit to Jan Wich) 39

Figure 5. Rex and his new girlfriend, Lieneke, argue about Saskia. (Credit to Anouk Sluizer) 60

Figure 6. Saskia is left alone in the car. (Credit to Anouk Sluizer) 67

Figure 7. Lemorne meets with Rex for the first time. (Credit to Anouk Sluizer) 92

Figure 8. Saskia and Rex are together for the final time. (Credit to Anouk Sluizer) 98

Figure 9. Behind the Scenes of *Spoorloos*' closing sequence. (Credit to Jan Wich) 113

Synopsis

George Sluizer's film *Spoorloos* follows a young Dutch couple, Rex Hofman (Gene Bervoets) and Saskia Wagter (Johanna ter Steege), on a summer cycling trip during the Tour de France. During a regular stop-off at a service station in rural France, Saskia disappears, seemingly, into thin air. This disappearance gives *Spoorloos* its title. In the UK and US, *Spoorloos* is widely known under the title *The Vanishing* and the literal translation of the original Dutch title into English is *Traceless* or *Without a Trace*.

While Rex fills the car tank, Saskia steps into the station to pick up refreshments. Disappearing into crowds of bustling holidaymakers, she never returns and is never seen again, with no reliable eyewitnesses to her disappearance. *Spoorloos* follows Rex's three-year-long obsessive search for Saskia. Memories of Saskia's disappearance haunt Rex. He recalls, again and again, one of their final conversations, which refers to the title of the original novella that inspired the film, published in 1984 by Dutch author Tim Krabbé. The original Dutch title of the novella, *Het Gouden Ei*, translates into English as *The Golden Egg*.

This title comes from a recurring dream that Saskia shares with Rex. In the dream, she imagines herself travelling alone through outer space, trapped in an odd and unsettling shape – a golden egg. She describes agonising loneliness, trapped in the egg with no hope of escape. (As Rex says to Saskia, 'You are locked in, you float alone forever.') This isolation is only interrupted by the appearance of 'another golden egg, far away' on the horizon, threatening to collide with her egg. Oddly symbolic and open to multiple interpretations, Saskia's dream foreshadows her disappearance. After Saskia vanishes from the gas station, the film cuts back and forth through a series of flashbacks and ellipses forward in time. This structure echoes the pattern of Rex's obsessive memories about Saskia. The first of these flashbacks shifts the film's focus to Saskia's abductor, Raymond Lemorne (Bernard-Pierre Donnadieu), and reveals his preparations to abduct an anonymous woman.

Spoorloos offers intimate access to Lemorne's life and is a character study of the film's antagonist. It shares an extensive portrait of its villain, portraying his sociopathy in a detailed and chilling fashion. Lemorne is a well-to-do family man with two young daughters, living a comfortable life as a high-school chemistry teacher.

Beneath the appearance of unremarkable normality, Lemorne realises early in his life that he is different from other people. He identifies himself as a 'sociopath,' capable of dangerous feats, regardless of their risk or extremity. A pivotal moment in his adult life occurs during a family holiday with his wife and two daughters when he saves the life of a child drowning in a rural river.

After hearing his daughter praise his heroism, he decides that his good deed is worthless, and 'her admiration [not] worth anything' unless he proves himself 'absolutely incapable of doing anything evil.' In other words, Lemorne subjects his own actions to a perverse form of reasoning and logic. If he is capable of a self-sacrificial act of goodness, he may be equally capable of the exact opposite – an extreme act of wickedness. His sociopathic impulses push him to test himself and prove that he is capable of 'the most horrible deed that [he] could envision right at that moment.' This act is a secret from the audience until *Spoorloos*' final moments. However, readers of this book who are yet to watch the film should be warned that this synopsis will reveal *Spoorloos*' twist ending in its closing paragraphs.

Spoorloos shows Lemorne prepare for this 'horrible deed.' These preparations include testing chloroform on himself, detailing its effects, and conducting several awkward abductions before successfully kidnapping Saskia. *Spoorloos* moves back and forth between Lemorne's exacting preparations and Rex's obsessive hunt for Saskia. The film takes an even more ominous turn after a media appeal by Rex, who affirms 'he is prepared to do anything' to know what happened to Saskia. Lemorne decides to meet Rex in Amsterdam with a unique offer. Rex can find out what happened to Saskia, but only by agreeing to travel with him to the site of her disappearance and to experience the same ordeal that she experienced.

Predictably, Rex's first instinct when meeting Lemorne face to face is to force him to reveal what happened to Saskia. He attacks him and threatens to report him to the police as Saskia's abductor. However, Lemorne retains the upper hand, telling him: 'You can kill me. I acknowledge your right to do so. I'll take the risk. But you'll never know what happened to Saskia. I'm banking on your curiosity.'

Lemorne and Rex take a long car drive from the Netherlands to France. Throughout the cross-border journey, Lemorne tells Rex of his motives and backstory and hints at what happened during Saskia's final ordeal. Rex goes so far as to ask Lemorne whether he raped Saskia. Lemorne is perplexed by the accusation, almost disappointed that Rex would not realise that his motives do not fit predictable sociopathic behaviour.

Rex finally arrives back at the gas station where Lemorne abducted Saskia. The site of Saskia's disappearance is highly symbolic. Lemorne is bringing Rex back to the site where the answers lie. He offers Rex a coffee drugged with a sleeping agent. If Rex takes the drug, he will know what happened to Saskia when he awakes. Again, Rex cannot resist his curiosity, so he drinks. Rex awakes to discover what Saskia endured in her final moments. He is underground, buried alive in a coffin, with no hope of rescue. With only his hand-held lighter, Rex has doomed himself to die alone with only the memory of Saskia to console him. Bright light fills the screen, echoing the shape of the titular golden egg and symbolising Rex's final moments. Rex's fate fulfils the macabre foreshadowing of Saskia's dream.

The final scene of *Spoorloos* shows Lemorne sitting in the garden of his rural holiday home. He sits above recently tilled ground where we assume he has buried Saskia and Rex. The front page of a newspaper sits at Lemorne's feet and reports on Rex's disappearance. With echoes of Saskia's abduction, it offers no clues as to how Rex has seemingly vanished into thin air. Saskia and Rex are reunited in a perverse twist of fate, and the mystery of the vanishing is solved by Rex willingly enduring Saskia's fate. Rex's curiosity has been satisfied at a dire and fatal cost.

Introduction: *Spoorloos* and International Success

At the 1989 Sydney Film Festival, a little-known independent film was a last-minute addition to the festival programme. Quite unexpectedly, it won the popular vote through the Sydney Film Festival Audience Award (*Spoorloos* DVD commentary, Criterion Collection, 2001). *Spoorloos* (1988), directed by French-born Dutch filmmaker George Sluizer, promptly won further international accolades. By the end of the first year of its release, *Spoorloos* had already picked up a slew of awards in Sluizer's home country. These awards included the Dutch Film Critics Award and the prestigious Golden Calf Award for Best Full-Feature Film at the Netherlands Film Festival.

Sluizer's female lead, the Dutch actress Johanna ter Steege, also won a Best Supporting Actress award in the first European Film Awards celebration held in the closing months of 1988 (British Film Institute, 1990). Beyond the Netherlands, *Spoorloos* attracted further attention when it was released under the title of *The Vanishing* and distributed to English-speaking audiences in 1991. Critics were impressed by *Spoorloos* and the film won international praise beyond European film festivals. The *New York Times*' Janet Maslin praised the 'spooky precision' of Sluizer's direction and described Spoorloos as 'building a disturbing horror story from these seemingly modest beginnings' (Maslin, 1991). At the same time, Roger Ebert described *Spoorloos* as a 'psychological jigsaw puzzle' that 'advances in a tantalizing fashion' with 'everything lead[ing] up to a climax that is as horrifying as it is probably inevitable' (Ebert, 1991).

As it totted up acclaim and awards, *Spoorloos* was even in with a running chance at an Oscar nomination. Critics briefly touted *Spoorloos* as a potential Dutch entry to the 61st Academy Awards (AMPAS) for Best Foreign Language Film. Eventually, it was only a technicality that excluded *Spoorloos* from a nomination. As a French–Dutch–West-German co-production, over 50 percent of *Spoorloos*' dialogue is in French. This dialogue defied the AMPAS's restrictive requirement that nominated films should be in the home language of the nominating country (Varndell, 2014: 38).[1]

Spoorloos continues to fascinate film fans and audiences many decades after its release. It has been described as an 'unforgettably chilling psychodrama' and as a 'sickly poetic' love story transformed into a horrifying tale of obsession (*Time Out*, 2012; Nayman, 2018). *Spoorloos* continues to feature in lists by magazines, including *Time Out* and *The Ringer*, cataloguing some of the scariest horror movie scenes in film history (Meares, 2021; De Semlyn and Rothkopf, 2023). Enthusiastic horror fans and film bloggers also offer colourful praise for the cult hit. The blogger writing under the pseudonym Persephone van der Waard writes:

> Like many Gothic tales, a strange element of fun lingers amid the hellish torment. It has all the ingredients of mystery and revenge: a boyfriend and his lover, wronged by a perfidious killer. But it lacks the mediaeval imagery and immediate fanfare of American outings (*Seven*, *Silence of the Lambs*, etc). Instead, it's more laid back – a vacation gone awry. (2020)

With its enduring success, *Spoorloos* has earned a highly respected reputation. It still holds the high regard that Stanley Kubrick expressed when he described it as 'the most terrifying film [he] had ever seen in his life' in a personal phone call with Sluizer (Alink, 2014). The film revolves around the disappearance of a young woman, Saskia Wagter (Johanna ter Steege), who seems to vanish into thin air during a holiday with her boyfriend, Rex Hofman (Gene Bervoets). The couple, on a cycling holiday in France during a hot summer, stop at a freeway service station. Saskia walks into the station to buy drinks and, without warning, disappears without a trace. Despite the efforts of police detectives, her whereabouts remain unknown. After three years, the case is considered cold, but Rex continues to search for Saskia.

New audiences may glance at the title and anticipate a conventional crime mystery or whodunit. The generic structure of the predictable crime film often features a crime, a pursuit of the perpetrator and a resolution. A typical whodunit opens with a crime. Detectives undertake a suspenseful search for the perpetrator, often against the clock, hoping to capture the criminal before they strike again. More often than not, the crime is solved by the perpetrator's capture.

However, Sluizer is not interested in the conventions of a typical mystery or whodunit film. Instead, *Spoorloos* introduces Saskia's abductor within the film's opening moments. Raymond Lemorne (played by French actor Bernard-Pierre Donnadieu) is an anonymous, middle-class professional and ordinary family man with two young daughters. The audience knows his identity from early in the film. Yet there is still no evidence to link him to an abduction. Saskia has vanished for good. The literal translation of the Dutch title *Spoorloos* into English is *Without a Trace* (British Film Institute, 1990). Rex is clueless: no one saw her disappear, and no trace of her remains after her disappearance.

Like many new viewers of *Spoorloos*, especially in the UK, I stumbled across the film on television rather than in the cinema. I first saw *Spoorloos* after watching select clips on the Channel 4 programme *100 Greatest Scary Moments* (2004). *Spoorloos* ranks number 55 on this list, which also features iconic horror films and is topped by Stanley Kubrick's *The Shining* (1980). By 2004, *Spoorloos*' twist ending had a well-known reputation that was heavily commented on in the programme commentary. Film critic Mark Kermode described the film as having one of the 'most heart-stopping climaxes' in recent film history, leaving him in a 'state of abject panic' ('The 100 Scariest Movie Moments No.55 "The Vanishing"'; Kermode and Mayo, 2020).

The cat-and-mouse relationship between Rex and Raymond Lemorne, Saskia's abductor, is one of the most memorable features of *Spoorloos*. As Kim Newman observes, 'We know, almost from the start, who did it. We know who the psycho is, but we don't know what he has done' (2001). Sluizer structures the film into three distinct phases. The first phase is the day of Saskia's disappearance and focuses on Rex and Saskia's relationship before the vanishing. The second phase focuses on the months immediately before Saskia's disappearance and depicts Lemorne's preparations for Saskia's abduction. The third phase overlaps and interweaves with the second phase and focuses on Rex's search for Saskia. This phase culminates with Rex's final face-to-face confrontation with Lemorne.

Lemorne is the sociopath hiding in plain sight. He is an unsettlingly normal individual. He is a villain in the model of Hannibal Lecter in Jonathan Demme's *The Silence of the Lambs* (1991) and other Thomas Harris adaptations. Like Hannibal Lecter, Lemorne is not an obvious villain or monster. He is a professional and intelligent person who has status within society. He may be a murderer, but he is highly urbane and sophisticated. Like the inscrutable Hannibal Lecter, Lemorne's appearance defies efforts to understand motives and patterns of behaviour. His harmless and normal appearance means those around him can never know who to trust and who to suspect.

Despite its villain and memorable twist ending, *Spoorloos* does not fit neatly into broader categories or genres of horror cinema. Reviewers repeatedly avoid describing *Spoorloos* as a horror film. Instead, they describe the film as a 'terrifying' or 'suspenseful' thriller and tend to avoid the horror label altogether. It is worth exploring this reception in further detail to understand how critics received *Spoorloos* following its release and how it has not been easily categorised as belonging to a specific genre or type of film.

SPOORLOOS: EARLY CRITICISM AND RECEPTION

Early reviews of *Spoorloos* interpreted the film's ability to horrify as an expression of Sluizer's unique artistic vision rather than an extension of the horror genre's familiar preoccupation with human evil and psychology. For instance, upon *Spoorloos*' immediate release in the Netherlands, the Dutch press immediately drew comparisons to Alfred Hitchcock. *De Telegraaf*, the largest Dutch daily newspaper, described the film as a 'brilliant thriller in the best tradition of the genre' and an 'ode to Hitchcock' ('What the Critics Have Said About *The Vanishing*'). Stephen J. Schneider and Kevin Sweeney recognise the limitations of this enthusiastic reception. In Schneider and Williams' edited collection on international horror traditions, they recall how 'the Dutch film community elected not to read [*Spoorloos*] as a genre picture at all, stressing instead its distinctive "artistic" and "intellectual" merits' (Schneider and Sweeney, 2005: 193).

This early criticism seems eager to claim Sluizer as the Netherlands' foremost director (hence the comparisons to Hitchcock). It is easy to see why this is an appealing angle. Dutch cinema is less prominent than other national traditions of European cinema. However, such emphatic praise has proved limiting for critical interpretations of *Spoorloos*. Indeed, this book argues that this early enthusiasm overshadowed a substantially more nuanced analysis of *Spoorloos*' contributions to genre cinema, and especially horror cinema.

A disdain for horror cinema is apparent from Schneider and Sweeney's overview of *Spoorloos*' early reception in their dedicated essay on Dutch 'thriller' cinema in the book *Horror International* (2005). Both authors refer to *The Hague*'s survey of 1988 Dutch film releases in their commentary. They recall how critics positively contrasted *Spoorloos* to a Dutch horror slasher film released the same year, *Amsterdamned* (1988). Dick Maas' *Amsterdamned* follows conventions of the type of slasher cinema popularised by franchises featuring *Halloween*'s invincible Michael Myers (1979), *Friday the 13th*'s vengeful Jason Voorhees (1980), and *A Nightmare on Elm Street*'s sadistic Freddy Krueger (1984). *Amsterdamned* follows the bloody trail of a serial killer prowling the famous canals of the iconic Dutch city for random victims.

Philip French describes *Amsterdamned* as a 'fast, gory, immensely entertaining horror flick that cleverly crosses *Dirty Harry* with *Jaws* and throws in a dash of *Don't Look Now*' (French, 2009). Reviewers negatively compared *Amsterdamned* to *Spoorloos* and welcomed Sluizer's film as a more sophisticated entry to Dutch cinema. These commentators described Sluizer's film as 'succeed[ing] without star actors, sex, horror or sensational speedboat stunts in the canals of Amsterdam.' *Spoorloos* was seen as offering 'a chilling plot' that contrasted with the 'mindless entertainment' in *Amsterdamned*. As a particularly icy review states, Sluizer's film, in contrast to *Amsterdamned*, 'demands some intellectual effort from his audiences' (Schneider and Sweeney, 2005: 193).

Such praise recognises *Spoorloos*' appeal. However, such comparisons dismiss horror as gore-splattered and formulaic entertainment incapable of originality. This assumption has led to unnecessarily narrow views of Sluizer's film. Instead, *Spoorloos* has multiple layers and interpretations. It is, first and foremost, a psychological horror with a shock twist ending. Psychological horror is a broad category of horror with a long history in cinema that overlaps with other genres, including thriller and film noir.

There are two sources of psychological horror in *Spoorloos*. First, there is the calculating sociopathy of Lemorne as its antagonist. Second, the film portrays Rex as a desperate and grieving man who will do nearly anything for closure. By Sluizer's own account, in an interview with Kermode after the film's release, *Spoorloos* explores the destructive potential of human obsession:

> It's not about evil – it's about the limits of how far you can go. […] A crucial line in the movie, which I find very important perhaps because it says something about myself runs something like: Perseverance can turn into obsession, and obsession can become senseless, dangerous. (Kermode, 1990)

Yet *Spoorloos* is also an exploration of grief as well as psychological horror. Sluizer's film depicts the transformation of Rex's raw loss into a duller, gnawing obsession that becomes more apparent and disturbing on repeat viewings. Viewers of *Spoorloos* frequently comment on this focus on grief, as evidenced by fan discussions on YouTube and film forums that dissect pivotal scenes (Plan-Séquence, 2022; *Little White Lies*, 2022). Again and again, viewers revisit similar questions about *Spoorloos*. Is the film's ending a nihilistic trick on the viewer, or does it have something profound to say about morbid obsession and loss?

Pundits are also keen to recognise this subtlety and distinguish *Spoorloos* from spectacle-orientated Hollywood cinema. One reviewer describes the horror in *Spoorloos* as coming from the 'fear of the unknown.' *Spoorloos* is also unnerving for its depiction of its central antagonist. The same reviewer notes Sluizer's 'insistence on not judging Raymond [Lemorne] in the film' and not shrouding his actions in melodramatic suspense ('The Most Terrifying Film?'). Steve Murray also asks: 'Remember Hitchcock's decision to reveal Kim Novak's true identity midway through Vertigo? *Spoorloos* is less interested in giving you a quick jolt than in planting seeds of unease that continue to sprout long after you leave the theatre' (cited in Schneider, 2002: 193).

This book is one of the first book-length studies to broaden these discussions and analyse *Spoorloos* in significant depth as a psychological horror film. This book argues that *Spoorloos* captures the adaptability of the horror genre as a mode of cinema that can blend psychological terror with grisly physical violence. The following chapters argue that *Spoorloos* is an especially memorable type of psychological horror film. *Spoorloos* foreshadows and adapts conventions that remain apparent in contemporary horror films, including films associated with the controversial 'post-horror' label such as *It Follows* (2014), *Hereditary* (2018), and *Speak No Evil* (2022). Taking a fresh look at *Spoorloos* and its enduring reputation, this book explores the film's emphasis on psychology and obsession.

Horror and Realism in *Spoorloos*

Spoorloos fits well into a genre described by Robin Wood, one of the early pioneers of horror film criticism, as 'the most disreputable of the genres' in popular culture (2018a: 63). While most commentary has resisted classifying *Spoorloos* as a straightforward horror film, this book focuses on how the film defies clichéd perceptions of horror cinema as extreme and sensationalist. Sluizer's filmmaking in *Spoorloos* is not readily reduced to a confrontational series of violent and shocking sequences. The film adopts an unchronological narrative with multiple perspectives and keeps horror within the confines of day-to-day life.

Spoorloos' style is characterised by a subtle, if pervasive, sense of unease that creeps up on its audience. Sluizer ranks lingering suspense and dread over direct scares. Perhaps the closest comparison to Sluizer's filmmaking is the work of the Austrian director Michael Haneke. Haneke's work is well known for focusing on claustrophobic domestic situations disrupted by instances of inexplicable violence. Haneke's most prominent film, *Funny Games* (1997), depicts the torture and murder of a French suburban family at their holiday home by two nameless male intruders.

The film's violence unfolds at an unnervingly slow and almost nonchalant pace at the hands of the anonymous perpetrators. The ending is a dark, gruesome twist that echoes *Spoorloos*' final moments. Critical assessments of Haneke's work echo assessments of the violence in *Spoorloos*. As Lisa Coulthard writes,

> Haneke's films since *Funny Games* do not address violence directly so much as they create an environment where one expects violence to erupt any second. Making violence pervasive, as if it is lying in wait, rather than exceptional, intrusive or surprising is crucial to understanding Haneke's violence and the way in which it works as cinematic and ethical critique. (2013: 181)

The horror in Haneke's *Funny Games* does not come from violence itself. Instead, Haneke's films depict relentless violence or blur the boundaries between suspense and violent action. As Coulthard observes, 'in this act of questioning, violence becomes a question or problem, rather than a clear-cut entity, event or action' (ibid.).

With echoes of Haneke, *Spoorloos* also adopts a comparable narrative emphasising realism over violence. Yet, there is a sinister undertone to the film that is dictated by the personality and behaviour of the sociopathic Lemorne. Lemorne's sense of self and psychology are palpably different from those of other people. As he will eventually tell Rex, 'You can find me listed in the medical encyclopaedias, under "Sociopath" in the new editions.' Donnadieu invests Lemorne with charm as well as cruelty, conveyed through small but noticeable behaviours. Viewers witness his extensive preparations for the abduction. Lemorne is dangerous not solely because he is responsible for Saskia's disappearance. He is dangerous because he can manipulate others, coercing Rex through words and tapping into Rex's desperate desire for knowledge.

Central to *Spoorloos*' narrative is the relationship between the science-teacher-turned-serial-killer Lemorne and the obsessive Rex. Midway through *Spoorloos*, Raymond, in response to continued public appeals by Rex, initiates contact with Rex. He sends Rex an anonymous postcard, to his home in Amsterdam, with an invitation to meet at a café in Nîmes, France. He promises that Rex will sit face to face with the man responsible for Saskia's disappearance. Lemorne's agenda is to watch Rex at close range and determine how much he can draw out and manipulate.

Rex and Lemorne are already forming a hostile yet intense bond. Rex argues with his new girlfriend, Lieneke, about responding to these postcards. Sluizer frames the shot so Raymond is always present in the background, haunting the boundaries of the frames in a way that explicitly shows that Lemorne is in control of the events he watches. Like Donnadieu's performance, these sequences are understated and restrained. They contrast with the high-adrenaline editing that audiences might expect in thriller or horror cinema. Though *Spoorloos* features fairly conventional editing, the framing of these shots is visually striking, reflecting the intense power imbalance that divides Lemorne and Rex.

The most stomach-churning demonstration of Lemorne's power comes in *Spoorloos*' closing sequences. Lemorne offers Rex a coffee drugged with a sleeping agent, promising him that, if he drinks, he will know what happened to Saskia when he awakes. The power of Lemorne's words is evident as Rex, after an intense indecision, decides he cannot resist Lemorne's offer and chooses to drink. While Saskia's fate may have unfolded off screen, we have no choice but to watch Rex relive and experience her final moments. When he awakes, he is underground, buried alive in a six-foot coffin as Lemorne entombs it beneath the soil. The viewer is exposed to a 180-degree view of the coffin's interior, and the camera fades down on Rex's hysterical screams, his fingers scrambling at its corners.

Figure 1. Lemorne makes his offer to Rex. (Credit to Anouk Sluizer)

This final moment in *Spoorloos* continues to rank highly in lists by *Rotten Tomatoes* and other outlets of memorable moments in cinema (Meares, 2021). Arthur Goyaz, writing in late 2023, described the film's ending as 'one of the most disturbing endings ever made' (2023). At the same time, commentators have begun to depart from the initial consensus that praised *Spoorloos* as a Hitchcockian-style thriller. Instead, growing efforts to integrate the film into a contemporary horror canon have become more vocal. Critics recognise that the gut-punching ending is not the sole moment of horror in *Spoorloos*. This trend is especially apparent in studies focusing on European horror cinema (for example, Dyer, 2015: 25 and Wynter, 2017: 51).

In his work on 'continental horror,' Kevin Wynter claims that *Spoorloos* had a transformative influence on European horror. He argues that the film 'offers a deeper look into the nature of the serial killer's violence' and 'anticipates many of the motifs that will come to define the continental horror film' of the 1990s and early 2000s (2017: 51). For Wynter, *Spoorloos* features memorable themes, including the dangers of curiosity, stranger danger, and the banality of evil, that are prominent parts of European or 'continental' horror cinema. This book aims to expand on this conclusion. Like any valuable film, themes within *Spoorloos* take on new meanings with every viewing. On repeat viewings, the personal story of Rex and Saskia offers disturbing insights into the role of random chance in human tragedy.

This book approaches *Spoorloos* as a film in which psychological horror, suspense, and even black comedy collide. *Spoorloos* still has a high-profile reputation, as evidenced by anniversary screenings, including the 2017 BFI Thriller on Tour in the UK. This book argues that this profile reflects the adaptability of horror cinema and conventions (BFI Thriller on Tour, 2017). Horror is a mode of cinema that, across diverse national traditions, blends psychological fears with existential terror and physical violence. The horror begins in *Spoorloos*' opening sequence when Saskia, driving along the freeway with Rex, tells of a dream that foreshadows her own death. 'My nightmare, I had it again last night.' The following chapters in this book explore how the film uses different conventions from the horror genre to convey unsettling ideas about morbid curiosity, grief, and obsession.

CHAPTER STRUCTURE

The final scene in *Spoorloos* may look like pure Gothic horror – painful, claustrophobic, and terrifying. However, the chapters in this book look beyond the film's ending. Instead, they examine *Spoorloos*' production, reception, and legacy in closer detail. Chapter One ('From Adaptation to Screen') briefly reviews the film's production history before its international success. This chapter provides crucial context to the book's analysis of Sluizer's film as a horror film. The chapter overviews Sluizer's career and summarises critical events in *Spoorloos*' production. These events provide insight into the challenges of independent filmmaking. They include the early development of the screenplay with Tim Krabbé, the author of the original novella, *The Golden Egg*.

Chapter One also retraces themes in *Spoorloos* to its source material in Krabbé's novella and draws on insights from Anne Sluizer, *Spoorloos*' producer and George Sluizer's spouse and long-term collaborator. Whilst detailing the novella's appeal as a book laced with bleak, existential symbolism and dark humour, the chapter also summarises *Spoorloos*' filming schedule, which was chequered by frequent logistical setbacks.

Building on this context, Chapter Two ('Lemorne, the Ordinary Everyman, and Psychological Horror') will then examine the critical reception of *Spoorloos*. It will discuss how *Spoorloos* remains a source of wary fascination for film critics and scholars, with its ability to defy genre labels. Despite its memorable finale, the film is frequently explored as 'one of the scariest non-horror movies ever made' and an antidote to graphic scares associated with horror cinema (Murray, 2014). In contrast to this criticism, Chapter Two recognises *Spoorloos* as a film that engages with human evil and monstrosity as critical themes in psychological horror cinema. It identifies *Spoorloos* as a psychological horror film that follows the now-popular model for horror films characterised by Robin Wood as the 'return of the repressed.'

Since Hitchcock's *Psycho* (1960), this 'return of the repressed' template has informed a significant strain of horror cinema. Wood argues that the monsters and villains of post-1960 horror cinema represent all desires that are repressed by the social order of 'monogamy and the family.' The monster is the release of 'an immense, hence very dangerous, surplus of sexual energy that will have to be repressed; what is repressed must always struggle to return in however disguised and distorted a form' (Wood, 2018a: 64). Lemorne, as *Spoorloos*' villain, represents these repressed desires that return as monstrous impulses and actions.

Chapter Three ('A Portrait of a Serial Killer') broadens the book's analysis to examine *Spoorloos* as part of the serial-killer sub-genre of horror cinema. This type of horror has become especially prominent through slasher films (*Halloween*, 1979; *Friday the 13th*, 1980) and slasher-rival films (*Scream*, 1996) between the 1970s and 1990s. Lemorne in *Spoorloos* represents multiple fears about the modern serial killer. He can move under the radar, even across borders and countries, and escape detection by the authorities. This chapter argues that *Spoorloos* reflects the popularisation of the serial killer in 1980s horror films. Sluizer's film depicts an antagonist linked to anxieties about law and justice and the limitations of both in a globalising modern world.

The following two chapters then turn to a growing body of work that re-evaluates *Spoorloos* and its influence on horror cinema. Chapter Four ('Grief and the Gothic in *Spoorloos*') argues that *Spoorloos* deftly transplants elements of the Gothic mode – as a mode of horror emphasising obsession and paranoia – onto the series of power games between Rex and Lemorne. What makes *Spoorloos* so horrifying is not Saskia's abduction but its exploration of the finality of death. This chapter argues that Gothic conventions are essential to this theme in *Spoorloos*.

Chapter Five ('*Spoorloos* as Post-horror Cinema') then builds on this argument. 'Post-horror' has become a key and, at times, controversial talking point in debates about horror cinema in the early decades of the millennium. While horror cinema is conventionally associated with excessive or supernatural threats, post-horror cinema frequently depicts psychological conflict and distress. This chapter will counteract arguments that post-horror cinema is a relatively new phenomenon. Instead, it will examine *Spoorloos* as an example of how horror cinema has consistently engaged with such psychological themes. *Spoorloos* captures the same spirit of post-horror cinema by questioning the limits of what is watchable and implicating the audience in intense ethical questions about obsession and knowledge. An account of *Spoorloos* would also be incomplete without referencing Sluizer's own controversial Hollywood remake of the film. This English-language version reversed these elements and had the opposite reception to that of his original film.

Chapter Six ('Adaptations and Transformations') examines Sluizer's Twentieth Century Fox remake, *The Vanishing* (1993). This American remake was panned for reversing the original's climax and was widely seen as an example of Hollywood's flawed appropriation of international cinematic traditions. The chapter will tap into timely debates about how international audiences see horror cinema by revisiting *The Vanishing*. Ultimately, this book aims to re-evaluate *Spoorloos* and to link its motifs to various horror sub-genres, including Gothic and psychological horror. *Spoorloos* deserves recognition for how it frames new motifs in a memorable way that expands the paradigms of the contemporary horror genre. Across these chapters, this book offers the first study of *Spoorloos* as a European horror film with a distinct and evolving legacy that still resonates in modern-day horror cinema.

Notes

1. This book will use the original Dutch title to refer to George Sluizer's 1988 film *Spoorloos*. The literal English translation of this word is 'traceless' or 'without a trace.' As I discuss in the Introduction and Chapter Six, this book will refer to Sluizer's 1993 English-language remake of his film as *The Vanishing*. Distributors and critics frequently use the title *The Vanishing* to promote Sluizer's original film to English-speaking audiences. Critics also have a tendency to refer to the original *Spoorloos* film as *The Vanishing*. However, this book will retain the original Dutch title to mark the specific boundaries between the two adaptations.

Chapter 1: From Adaptation to Screen

Spoorloos remains a source of wary fascination for film critics and scholars who have yet to build a consensus on the film's genre. Scott Foundas' essay, released as part of the 2014 Criterion edition, observes the compelling and 'richly philosophical darkness' at the film's heart. Foundas describes Spoorloos as 'a dark, mythic fable' and 'deceptively simple in design […] forcing Rex – and us – to choose between eternal ignorance and knowledge that comes at an undisclosed price' (2014). However, behind the film's layered symbolism is a more predictable production history for an independent film with a limited budget.

Production began with Sluizer's co-drafting of the screenplay with Tim Krabbé, the author of the original novella, *The Golden Egg*. Certain parts of *Spoorloos* should be familiar to readers of Krabbé's short, memorable book. Krabbé's tightly structured novella alternates between Rex and his efforts to find out the cause of Saskia's disappearance and Raymond Lemorne as he plans the disappearance. *The Golden Egg* offers intimate access to Lemorne's life and is a character study of its antagonist. This focus turns the predictable 'whodunit' formula into a more probing – and disturbing – look at the darker side of human psychology.

Krabbé's plain, descriptive prose gives the illusion of offering a macabre look at the thought processes of a potential killer. Lemorne is calculating and methodical, and even the moment of Saskia's abduction is described in brutally concise sentences:

> With a wild gasp she turned away from him; Lemorne bent his arm and covered her face with his hand, tensed and forceful. She arched her back like a high diver about to take the plunge. Then she let her drinks drop and slide down into the seat. Gotcha, thought Lemorne. (Krabbé, 2003: 80)

The chilling effect of this narration is to normalise even the most disturbing of actions. This is the effect that Matt Seaton recognises when he compares Krabbé to the American novelist Patricia Highsmith, the author of psychological thrillers *Strangers on a Train* (1950) and *The Talented Mr Ripley* (1955). 'Like [Highsmith],' Seaton writes, 'his stories are tightly plotted, with strong characters and acute observation of social mores and individual psychology. But Krabbé's [works] also have a more European, existentialist sense of the absurd – as if his characters dimly perceive themselves as victims of some bleak cosmic joke' (2003).

With a varied set of work, Krabbé has become one of the Netherlands' prominent authors. He is well known to Dutch readers for *De Renner* (*The Rider*, 1978). This semi-autobiographical novel is now described as a 'classic of sports literature.' It recounts in 'dark, compelling prose the pain and glory involved in a fictional race' based on the Tour de France (Usborne, 2015). Critics frequently recognise Krabbé's other works, including *Red Desert Penitentiary* (1975) and *Die Grotte* (*The Cave*, 1997), as formulaic thrillers or mystery novels. However, his books are more innovative and unpredictable than these generic labels. They often feature morally troubling characters confronting rather bleak and existentialist situations.

SLUIZER'S FILMOGRAPHY

This existentialism first attracted Sluizer to the prospect of adapting *The Golden Egg*. Seaton describes *Spoorloos* as a 'brooding, melancholic' story 'that might come from a newspaper clipping.' However, 'precisely where the wellspring of his fiction is to be found, Krabbé is not eager to speculate about' (2003). Interestingly, Krabbé was a long-term acquaintance of Sluizer. Krabbé's mother, the film translator Margreet Reiss, was a Dutch language tutor for Anne Sluizer, George Sluizer's wife and producer. Sluizer was the director of the film adaptation of Krabbé's *Red Desert Penitentiary* (1985). Sluizer's adaptation tells the story of a protagonist (James Michael Taylor) who claims to have been held captive for 20 years in a one-room cell in the US southwestern desert. The film casts doubt on the truthfulness of narratives and settings. Its viewers are left unsure whether they are witnessing the protagonist's actual ordeal or the private hallucinations of a man driven to the brink by his demons.

Anne Sluizer, as a producer of *Red Desert Penitentiary* as well as *Spoorloos*, has fond memories of *Red Desert Penitentiary*'s production. 'It was a very special production and we very much enjoyed making it – with almost nothing but wonderful people, in Sweetwater, Texas, where George had also shot a documentary about rattlesnakes

(*Sweetwater Junction*, 1981)' (Sluizer, 2023). Anne Sluizer's reference to this documentary alludes to Sluizer's wider filmography, which moves between a range of genres. Sluizer's career certainly does not fit the conventional mould of a horror or psychological thriller director.

A brief overview of Sluizer's filmmaking career may provide helpful context here. It is useful to recap Sluizer's filmography and consider how it resists efforts to identify his work with marketable film genres. After studying at the *L'Institut des hautes études cinématographiques* (Paris, IDHEC), Sluizer's first production was the documentary *Hold Back the Sea* (*De Lage Landen*, 1961). This wide-ranging documentary addresses Holland's five-century struggle with rising sea levels and won the Silver Bear Award at the Berlin Film Festival in 1961. Sluizer's later filmography included National Geographic documentaries alongside Dutch dramas that gained recognition through European film festival circuits.

Later documentaries demonstrate a sustained interest in bringing unlikely topics to new audiences. They include features on Portuguese cod fishermen in Greenland (*Lonely Doryman*, 1968) and the 1970 Holland Pop Festival headlined by Pink Floyd (*Stamping Ground*, 1970). Sluizer also filmed a documentary in Ireland that included footage of President John F. Kennedy's final visit to the Republic of Ireland, ten days before his assassination in 1963. Writers such as Peter Verstraten have praised the breadth of this filmography. Verstraten describes one of Sluizer's later films, *João en het mes*, as a 'stunning debut feature' (2016: 13).

João en het mes (translated as *João and the Knife*) was shot in Brazil ahead of its 1972 release. Beginning with *João en het mes*, Sluizer has consistently ventured into darker thematic territory. It featured a Brazilian cast and focuses on João (Jofre Soares), who is married to a much younger wife (Ana Maria Miranda). After leaving for a long absence, João is tormented by the possibility of infidelity and decides to kill his wife rather than live with doubt and lack of trust. The film foreshadows themes in *Spoorloos*. *João en het mes* probes taboo subjects, focusing on characters grappling with obsession and desire for control.

Since this debut feature, Sluizer has shown consistent interest in narratives that centre on the theme of obsessive control. In the documentary *Sluizer Speaks* (2014), Sluizer describes *João en het mes* as a film about doubt and the extent to which people can live with doubt (Alink, 2014). The film tracks how unsettling doubt becomes a destructive obsession in its protagonist. Across his filmography, including *Spoorloos*, Sluizer's protagonists are plagued by self-sabotaging tendencies that turn grief or doubt into obsession. In Sluizer's thriller *Twice a Woman* (1979), voyeuristic desire similarly morphs into obsession.

This transformation in *Twice a Woman* begins when a divorced museum director (Bibi Andersson) is caught up in a love triangle. The director falls for a much younger woman (Sandra Dumas) and discovers the woman is also having an affair with her ex-husband (Anthony Perkins). Such plots lend themselves to melodrama. Indeed, Hans Van Driel describes *Twice a Woman* as a film that 'broke new ground' as a literary adaptation of a novel by the Dutch author Harry Mulisch. 'It attracted large audiences,' Van Driel writes, and Sluizer was praised for 'emphasising the melodramatic aspect of Mulisch's novel, namely the vicissitudes between woman, girl and man, skilfully weaving them into engrossing cinema' (Van Driel, 2004: 155).

Sluizer also cast Perkins in *Twice a Woman*, the actor responsible for the iconic Norman Bates in Alfred Hitchcock's watershed horror *Psycho* (1960). This choice fits Sluizer's body of work, which, at significant points in his filmography, focuses on the darker side of the human psyche. Sluizer himself acknowledges that he sees unnerving and disturbing an audience as a 'function of cinema.' He observes in a promotional interview for *Spoorloos* that he 'does [his] best to provoke, to magnify situations and characters in such a way that the audience would be disturbed because we have to recognise in ourselves the potential for evil' (Cordiay, 1989: 43).

Like Sluizer's previous films, *Spoorloos* gets under an audience's skin by depicting the horrific possibilities lurking within the circumstances of ordinary life. It may have been this sense of the everyday horrific that first attracted Sluizer to Krabbé's novella *The Golden Egg*. According to Anne Sluizer, George Sluizer knew of *The Golden Egg*'s manuscript before it was published and was intrigued by its premise (Sluizer, 2023). However, despite having worked together on the film adaptation of Krabbé's *Red Desert Penitentiary* (1985), their collaboration on *Spoorloos* was fraught. After purchasing the novella's film rights, Sluizer approached three screenwriters to draft a film synopsis for discussion with Krabbé. No version of the script was to Krabbé's satisfaction. Sluizer allowed Krabbé to write the screenplay himself. However, Sluizer was dissatisfied with this first draft and found this version of the script too uncinematic due to being too 'bound, in the timing and the rhythm, to literature' (Cordiay, 1989: 43).

> [Krabbé's] first draft was not bad, but it was not good. So, I suggested that we write the second draft together. Which we did followed by the third draft. On the third draft, we had different opinions about […] the placing of scenes and the way to tell a story from a film point-of-view rather than a literary point-of-view. (Alink, 2014)

Sluizer parted from Krabbé after successive arguments and finished the final screenplay before the first day of an eight-week shoot beginning in September 1987. Sluizer's screenplay offers a non-linear take on Krabbé's novella. It reorders the narrative to heighten tension at pivotal moments and build a gruelling type of suspense that makes the horror of the final scene even more stark and dramatic.

Figure 2. George Sluizer and Johanna ter Steege on the Spoorloos *set. (Credit to Jan Wich)*

Despite being shot for a modest $165,000 across France and the Netherlands, the production of *Spoorloos* was not without its challenges. The strain of this production led to some memorable clashes on the film set. It is worth noting that the film's eventual success was not a foregone conclusion during pre-production. The coming together of the central cast for the on-location shoot was a result of luck and chance, underscoring the unpredictable nature of independent filmmaking.

Casting and Filming *Spoorloos*

In an article for *Total Film* featuring interviews with Sluizer, Krabbé, and lead actor Gene Bervoets, Matt Glasby writes in detail about the filming process for *Spoorloos*. He observes that '[p]erhaps the greatest mystery of this methodical puzzle that slots awfully, inexorably, into place was that (almost) no one was hurt during filming' (2016: 104). The filming began predictably enough. Sluizer made decisions based on instinct rather than a rigorous audition process. Sluizer cast Johanna ter Steege as Saskia, then an unknown actor in the final years of drama school in Kampen, Netherlands.

Sluizer invited ter Steege to audition after a tip-off from a casting director. As Sluizer recalls, '[she] had one advantage. She had red hair, blonde-red hair, and I wanted Saskia to have more or less the colour of the hair of my own daughter' ('Interview – George Sluizer'). The casting of Saskia's partner, Rex, was equally spontaneous. Sluizer cast Gene Bervoets as Rex due to his one slight advantage over another rival actor. Bervoets was able to speak both Flemish Dutch and French.

Casting Raymond Lemorne was a more complicated business. The original actor Sluizer wished for Lemorne was Jean-Louis Trintignant, a prominent French actor with credits in films by Bernardo Bertolucci, François Truffaut, and Michael Haneke. However, Trintignant was unavailable for the year of *Spoorloos*' shooting. Sluizer remembered Bernard-Pierre Donnadieu, an extra from his previous film with Anthony Perkins, *Twice a Woman* (1979). He describes Donnadieu as 'this extra, who came from nowhere and played a little part […] I remembered how his character threw a cigarette he was smoking. And I said to myself, that is someone who can put a whole character by throwing a cigarette away' ('Interview – George Sluizer').

Sluizer auditioned and cast Donnadieu after one meeting. With the cast in place, filming began in the Gard department of southern France, in and around the city of Nîmes and its Place aux Herbes, as well as the Marguerittes commune, east of Nîmes. Problems began on set with Donnadieu, whom Bervoets describes as acting 'like a dictator on set' (quoted in Glasby, 2016: 104). Sluizer was finally forced to confront Donnadieu during pre-production rehearsals as he repeatedly clashed with ter Steege. In her own 2014 interview released with *Spoorloos*' Criterion edition, ter Steege recalls a fraught relationship with Donnadieu due to her novice acting experience. She recalls Donnadieu's 'very strong personality.' She also describes him as 'insecure about me playing the part because he had never seen my work and he was very afraid that I was not good enough to [play] opposite him' ('Interview – Johanna ter Steege').

Figure 3. Bernard-Pierre Donnadieu on the Spoorloos *set. (Credit to Jan Wich)*

Johanna ter Steege threatened to walk away from the role of Saskia before Sluizer intervened to curtail Donnadieu's behaviour. Donnadieu's temper also frayed relationships with the crew and the cast. In Sluizer's own words, Donnadieu 'became a nuisance to the cameraman,' berating him for using dimmed lighting on set and underexposing the actors (Alink, 2014). The cameraman's refusal to work with Donnadieu forced Sluizer to find an emergency replacement for the final days of the shoot.

The on-set drama left its mark on the actors. Glasby quotes Sluizer in his profile: 'I needed people who could open the door to hell and not be afraid to step over the line' (2016: 104). However, nearly 30 years after the filming, the remaining cast and crew now see their experiences on the set of *Spoorloos* as generating a remarkable film. Even Krabbé, who did not attend the *Spoorloos* premiere after parting ways with Sluizer while writing the screenplay, was satisfied by the success.

Krabbé asked to see the film with Anne Sluizer after the positive press coverage that greeted *Spoorloos*' release. Anne Sluizer recalls Krabbé's gushing praise: 'Tell your husband that his film is better than my book' (Sluizer, 2023). While we only have Anne Sluizer's recollections to verify this statement, we also have evidence of other cast members praising the film. This praise from cast members also focuses on the moment of terror immortalised in the film's final take. Gene Bervoets, speaking at an anniversary screening at the International Film Festival in Rotterdam, recalled preparations for the claustrophobic final scene. He described Sluizer and Donnadieu boarding him into a coffin and covering it with sandbags to blot out any light. As he recalls: 'I could feel the sand covering my face. I got into a panic. And I'm sure in *Kill Bill*, I don't know whether it's in 1 or 2, the scene where Tarantino buries Uma Thurman alive, he simply pinched that from [Sluizer]' (Alink, 2014).

Even for the cast, the twist ending in *Spoorloos* continues to haunt and disturb. This is unsurprising. Martina Plock, among others, argues that taphephobia (the fear of being buried alive) is the most terror-inducing trope of the Gothic imagination. Such horrific imagery – muffled screams, hands clawing at sealed coffin lids – taps into a 'particular kind of phobic experience.' Scholars have retraced this phobia to 'Victorian writers who contributed to the making of the Gothic canon: Edgar Allan Poe, Charles Dickens, and Wilkie Collins' (Mangham, 2010: 6). Indeed, the primal fear of re-awakening in a sealed coffin continues to fuel crime films, thriller television serials, and horror cinema.

Spoorloos joins a range of psychological thrillers, including *Casino* (Martin Scorsese, 1995) and *Double Jeopardy* (Bruce Beresford, 1999), that feature the prospect of being buried alive. It also joins film and television serials that feature premature burial, including *Buried Alice* (Frank Darabont, 1990) and *Buried* (Rodrigo Cortés, 2010). However, *Spoorloos*' final scene is not the only memorable scene of horror in Sluizer's film. A pervasive and understated horror seeps into multiple scenes in *Spoorloos*. Like any memorable film, *Spoorloos* reveals new meanings with every viewing and the film blooms when its many layers are peeled away. *Spoorloos*' emphasis on psychology defies frankly clichéd perceptions of horror cinema. The disturbing personal story of Rex and Saskia becomes a more multi-layered narrative when it intersects with the film's antagonist, Lemorne. *Spoorloos* engages with the idea of human evil and, by placing the audience close to Lemorne's story, puts them in the unusual position of seeing parts of the story unfold from his perspective.

Spoorloos is the subject of increasing academic commentary, with only some of this criticism recognising the film's appeal as a horror film. The following chapter, 'Lemorne, the Ordinary Everyman, and Psychological Horror,' examines how *Spoorloos* is undergoing this critical re-evaluation. The chapter reviews the growing body of criticism that describes *Spoorloos* as an 'under-remembered masterpiece of horror filmmaking' (Cheded, 2018). In particular, it examines *Spoorloos* as a psychological horror film that centres upon the ordinariness of its main antagonist. This is a feature that became prevalent in 1980s and 1990s horror cinema and links closely to the sub-genre of serial-killer cinema that Chapter Three explores. This next chapter lays the foundation for Chapter Three by examining the eerie characteristic of ordinariness that Lemorne personifies in *Spoorloos*. This characteristic connects Lemorne, as *Spoorloos*' villain, to a prevalent character type that appears across successive phases of horror cinema, especially since Alfred Hitchcock's watershed *Psycho* (1960).

Chapter 2: Lemorne, the Ordinary Everyman, and Psychological Horror

Psychology and psychological horror are at the heart of *Spoorloos*. The human mind's negative emotions (obsession, guilt, and paranoia, in this instance) lead to the central character's downfall. The horror in Sluizer's film cannot be traced back to a supernatural threat. Instead, it ensues from a seemingly harmless everyday man masking interior evil. In the opening shots, *Spoorloos* begins with an innocuous road trip. A Dutch couple are on a cross-continental cycling holiday. The roof of their car is laden with bicycles. They practise their French vocabulary and bicker about the waning gas levels in the car as they move from the freeway onto quieter country tracks. The camera drifts between the car interior and the rural French countryside in these opening shots. The meandering roads complement the calm reassurance of human life on the move. There are few clues as to what kind of film *Spoorloos* will be.

For some viewers, the establishing shot of the couple's car echoes Stanley Kubrick's *The Shining* (1980) as they drive deeper into the peaceful countryside. This shot echoes the brooding, bird-of-prey shot that tracks Jack Torrance and his family's car journey to the infamous Overlook Hotel (Nayman, 2018). However, regardless of how helpful this comparison to Kubrick's iconic horror film would be for this book, I do not see significant similarities between the opening sequences of *Spoorloos* and *The Shining*. Kubrick's distant overhead shot, complete with Wendy Carlos and Rachel Elkind's dissonant score, almost immediately generates a sense of impending dread.

By contrast, there is a reassuring intimacy to our introduction to Saskia and Rex in *Spoorloos*. The film opens with a view of the anonymous countryside, with a grasshopper twitching in the foreground of the establishing shot. The camera swings over the red rooftops of a small hamlet adjacent to a busy highway. The shot pans over the traffic as Saskia's animated voiceover, chattering to Rex, pierces the shot. This opening scene captures the understated realism of the film. This realism is fitting since the horror in *Spoorloos* focuses on everyday life and the rupturing of peaceful everyday life by a dark, irreversible event. While introducing Saskia and Rex as a couple, the opening sequence for *Spoorloos* also introduces us to Raymond Lemorne. He sits in his car in the forecourt of a gas station, seemingly at daybreak before other travellers arrive. For now, he is an anonymous character, but his cunning duplicity is evident as he puts an arm cast over a healthy arm. Lemorne is certainly not what he seems.

Viewers may be able to grasp allusions to the real-life serial killer Ted Bundy. Bundy similarly adopted the arm cast to pretend to be injured and in need of help to lull his victims into a false sense of security. Lemorne's deception also foreshadows the tactics of the Buffalo Bill killer, Jame Gumb, in *The Silence of the Lambs* (Jonathan Demme, 1991). Gumb famously abducts Catherine Martin by luring her away from her apartment with this same tactic. While Lemorne has yet to meet Saskia or Rex, this short opening scene prepares us for a pivotal encounter in *Spoorloos*.

Coming face to face with a monster is a frequent and expected occurrence in horror cinema. Monstrosity has many guises. Mark Jancovich reminds us that 'different groups will represent the monstrous in different ways and representations will develop historically' (1994: 9). For many horror film experts, monstrosity is a physical characteristic. Films labelled 'body horror' or 'biological horror' in the style of John Carpenter's *The Thing* (1982), David Cronenberg's *The Fly* (1986), or Clive Barker's *Hellraiser* (1987) are characterised by an 'extreme level of gruesome disregard for the human body' (Cruz, 2012: 161).

Spoorloos is on the opposite end of this scale, eschewing gore and jump scares. Lemorne's sociopathic behaviour and his psychology, rather than his body or appearance, are the film's primary sources of horror. His behaviour defies ethical limitations on extreme and destructive behaviour. Noël Carroll's influential *The Philosophy of Horror* (1990) understands the significance of this 'cognitive' or psychological threat. Carroll writes that 'monsters are not only physically threatening; they are cognitively threatening. […] For such monsters are, in a certain sense, challenges to the foundations of a culture's way of thinking' (1990: 34).

With his reserved and observant temperament and bookish glasses, Lemorne is an unassuming character. He is the type of 'cognitive threat' who, in the words of Krabbé as *The Golden Egg's* original author, is a 'philosophical killer' who approaches his task with clinical perseverance (quoted in Glasby, 2016). Thus, from the moment he is introduced in the opening sequences, Lemorne is at the heart of a network of characters and relationships that tie the film together.

Lemorne has a contradictory status in *Spoorloos* – he is repellent yet fascinating. Sabine Vanacker describes this fascination in further detail. She writes that *Spoorloos*' 'thrill' does 'not stem from simple audience identification with a threatened hero. In fact, for the audience, the film acquires a frightening aspect because of our more likely identification with a fairly sympathetic baddy, the kidnapper, murdered and self-styled sociopath Raymond' (Vanacker, 1995: 97).

Throughout the film, Lemorne is made distinct by his everyday ordinariness. He is an everyday family man with a wife and two children, a modern professional, and a man who can blend into a crowd. Lemorne first sees Rex and Saskia from a distance as they arrive at the freeway gas station. He observes all comings and goings, pretending to be occupied by his newspaper as he scouts for a potential victim. We do not yet know his intentions, but we know that his anonymous appearance can help him disappear as needed. As vehicles, including large lorries, move in and out of shot, Lemorne is frequently blocked from our view.

Spoorloos' plot turns on Lemorne's eerie brand of ordinariness. He has a chameleon-like cunning and adaptability that can, again and again, evade detection. If any animal-like metaphor were to suit Lemorne, it would be insect-like or reptilian. Commentators have compared Lemorne's chameleon-like nature to an insect captured in *Spoorloos*' opening shot. The insect blends into a branch within the grassland alongside the freeway, which Rex and Saskia drive along at the start of their trip (Rafter, 2006: 99). This respectability is the essential cover for Raymond. A recurrent emphasis on Raymond's approachability is pivotal to *Spoorloos*. This emphasis on Lemorne's ordinary appearance is pivotal to *Spoorloos* since, as the audience will see in the film's closing scenes – and as this book will discuss in later chapters – it is this trait that encourages Saskia to let down her guard.

Lemorne's reassuring ordinariness is also central to his relationship with the obsessive Rex, as the closest character that *Spoorloos* has to a hero or a protagonist. In a later scene where the two men first meet, Lemorne taunts Rex by emphasising that he can reveal his identity without endangering himself. He coldly reminds Rex that he has no proof of his involvement in Saskia's disappearance and that no one would suspect a mild-mannered science teacher. When crossing the French border, Rex can even glimpse Lemorne's passport, including his home address. Lemorne is confident he cannot be linked to Saskia: 'True, I don't like the idea of you knowing my name. I have to limit my risks. But you could have traced [my address] from my license plate. You won't gain anything by opening an investigation. You have nothing on me.'

Sluizer structures the film around Rex's intensive efforts to discover the cause of Saskia's disappearance. Rex's obsessive search catches Lemorne's eye, and he observes him from afar. Lemorne taunts him with anonymous postcards that promise to reveal Saskia's whereabouts. Rex's exasperated new girlfriend warns him: 'He's playing with you. He's followed you through the papers and wants to see how far you'll go.' Lemorne and Rex are both characterised by obsession. Many films and genres, and especially thriller films, feature obsession and focus on protagonists who fixate on perfection. These films often depict the dark side of sacrificing everything, even one's essential humanity, to pursue perfection.

Such thrillers would include Georges Franju's *Eyes Without a Face* (*Les Yeux sans visage*, 1960) and its depiction of the obsessive Dr. Génessier, who is determined to restore the disfigured face of his once-beautiful daughter after a dramatic car accident. They would also include Brian De Palma's film fittingly titled *Obsession* (1976), which adapts themes from Hitchcock's *Vertigo* in a plot that features a New Orleans businessman infatuated with a woman who is the image of a long-dead wife who was killed years earlier in a fatal kidnapping incident.

Obsession is also a highly familiar theme in Hitchcock's thrillers, and plenty of the director's films, including *Marnie* (1964), feature the destructive effects of a past trauma upon a love affair. Scholars have studied *Marnie* as a touchstone film that captures recognisable features of the Hitchcock thriller. *Marnie* features Tippi Hedren as the eponymous heroine, whose life has been punctured by inexplicable psychotic episodes, and Sean Connery as the man who attempts to get to the root of her problems and discover the origins of her trauma in her earlier life. Charles Derry describes this plot as characteristic of the 'psychotraumatic thriller,' a sub-genre of the thriller film with conventions that include 'the heroine's involvement in a series of ongoing crimes as a result of a past trauma; her lack of awareness of the cause of the trauma [...] and her reenactment of the original trauma through a climatic flashback' (1988: 207).

The obsession in these psychological thrillers is self-destructive and unquenchable in ways that foreshadow Rex's obsession after Saskia's abduction. However, the depiction of Rex's obsession in *Spoorloos* is counterbalanced by the calculating sociopathy of Raymond Lemorne. Lemorne's obsession is different. His obsession does not render him powerless, but rather, it amplifies his abilities. He will go to extreme measures to prove he is capable of the most evil deed he can imagine. Rex, by contrast, is a disturbed and grieving man who will do nearly anything for closure. The relationship between the two men becomes closer throughout the film. Even in scenes focusing on Rex, *Spoorloos*' flashbacks return, again and again, to focus on Lemorne.

Midway through *Spoorloos*, in response to continued media appeals by Rex, Lemorne sends Rex an anonymous postcard, to his home in Amsterdam, with an invitation to meet at a café in Nîmes, France. He promises that Rex will sit face to face with the man responsible for Saskia's disappearance. Lemorne's agenda is to watch Rex at close range and determine how much he can draw out and manipulate. As Rex argues with his girlfriend about responding to these postcards, the shot is framed so Lemorne is consistently present in the background. Lemorne haunts the boundaries of the frames in a way that explicitly shows that he is in control of the events he watches. These sequences, although unnerving, are typically still and restrained. They contrast with high-adrenaline editing audiences might expect in thriller cinema. Though *Spoorloos* features conventional editing, the framing of these shots reflects the intense power imbalance that divides Lemorne and Rex.

In their first face-to-face meeting, Lemorne taunts Rex almost immediately. He homes in on Rex's Achilles heel – a near-self-destructive desire to know what happened to Saskia: 'Come with me to France and you'll know everything. I offer you this unique chance.' Lemorne's ordinariness is his protection. However, his capacity for evil becomes more profound when compared with Rex's self-destructive obsession, which, in turn, illustrates how easily people psychologically unravel under pressure. Even when Rex lashes out at Lemorne, he is not dissuaded from rubbing salt into the wound.

Lemorne emphasises how only he can unlock the mystery of Saskia's disappearance: 'I'm warning you, I've taken precautions. If anything happens to me, if you speak to anyone, my offer's no longer valid. And you won't know a thing!'

Lemorne is an ordinary man with a dark, destructive secret – a character type which is a familiar villain in horror cinema. He blends into the decisively modern world of *Spoorloos*' opening scenes – motorway traffic, urban travel, and tourism. Lemorne's place within *Spoorloos*' storytelling warrants further consideration within the context of horror cinema, especially psychological horror cinema. A closer examination of *Spoorloos*' antagonist and his psychology is essential to understanding *Spoorloos* as a horror film.

Psychological Horror:
From *Psycho* (1960) to *Spoorloos*

Psychological horror, a genre with distinctive origins, has evolved significantly over the late-twentieth century. This sub-genre can be traced through successive phases of cinema, overlapping with other types of cinema, including thriller and suspense films. In their 1972 study of horror cinema, Roy Hunter and T.J. Ross divided the horror genre into three overlapping yet distinct categories: 'gothic horror, monster terror, and psychological thriller' (quoted in Kawin, 2012: 210). While the first two categories often focus on supernatural threats, 'psychological thrillers' foreground their characters' internal lives and fears. More than most other genres, these films bring an audience face to face with negative aspects of human psychology in ways that reflect their fears and paranoia, thereby reflecting the complexities and nuances of the human experience.

Charles Derry expresses this most eloquently in his psychological history of the modern horror film:

> Certainly, horror films connect with our profound and subconscious needs to deal with the things that frighten us. In the way they work upon us, films are much like dreams, and horror films are like nightmares. Some horror films deal with our fears more directly than others, but in general, horror films speak to our subconscious and – as do our dreams – deal with issues that are often painful for us to deal with consciously and directly. (2009: 21)

Early psychological horror can be traced back to pre-war 1930s cinema in films including Tod Browning's *Freaks* (1932) and Edgar G. Ulmer's eerie *The Black Cat* (1934). These films intensify suspense through implied terrors rather than real-world monsters. As a film with the same name as the famous Edgar Allan Poe short story, the latter retains an 'ambiguity […] as to whether the supernatural comes into play or is merely an illusion engendered by a disturbed mentality' (Joshi, 1999: vi).

However, a more precise, mid-century shift in American cinema broadened the remit of these early psychological horror films. These films combined the excess of these earlier horror films with a modern type of psychological suspense focusing on antagonists' internal lives and pathologies. Alfred Hitchcock's *Psycho* (1960) was pivotal to the growth of this sub-genre and connected horror to the psychology of a seemingly everyday man. In the first essay he published, Robin Wood famously noted that *Psycho* redirected horror away from supernatural threats towards internal psychological conflict.

Psycho, Wood writes, 'makes an impression on our subconscious whether we are familiar with psychology or not' (2018c: 27). In case we need to recap the infamous story, *Psycho*'s heroine, Marion Crane (Janet Leigh), tumbles into the Bates Motel while on the run after stealing $40,000 from her workplace. Norman Bates (Anthony Perkins) seems timid and pliable and lives under his mother's thumb. The villain of *Psycho* is Bates' multiple personality disorder (MPD). Bates has absorbed the character traits of his long-dead and once-overbearing mother. He infamously keeps her corpse in the cellar whilst murdering Marion and others under the guise of his mother's personality.

If the attic represents Bates' stunted 'mental development,' then 'the cellar is the source of repressed sexuality: it is where we find the mother' (Wood, 2018c: 27). With this statement, Wood coined the now-popular model for horror films that he characterised as the 'return of the repressed.' Within this theory, the villain or monster in the horror film symbolises the desires, the danger, and the excess that have been suppressed beneath the hierarchies of society, including the monogamous nuclear family. The monster is the release of 'an immense, hence very dangerous, surplus of sexual energy that will have to be repressed; what is repressed must always struggle to return in however disguised and distorted a form' (Wood, 2018b: 79).

As with many theories concerning horror cinema, this phrase can be traced back to Sigmund Freud. In his essay *Beyond the Pleasure Principle* (1920), he expands on the nature of repression, writing that 'the patient cannot remember the whole of what is repressed in him, and what he cannot remember may be precisely the essential part of it. He is obliged to repeat the repressed material as a contemporary experience instead of remembering it as something in the past' (2003: 12).

Powerful sexual impulses lie dormant in the unconscious mind and tend to erupt or reappear in violent behaviour. According to Wood, the villain or monster in the horror film symbolises these sexual impulses. These impulses lurk beneath the surface and undermine the status quo, often threatening to rip it apart. The monster unleashes these repressed desires, and horror cinema is a genre that releases the 'necessary frustration, anxiety and neuroticism of our culture' (Wood, 2018b: 99). Norman Bates is the human monster who represents a 'return of the repressed' in horror cinema. He poses a threat to this dominant, normative order by subverting gender roles and societal boundaries.

Most persuasive accounts of horror cinema follow Wood's lead, recognising *Psycho* as providing fresh direction for horror cinema. As Paul Wells sees it, *Psycho* was 'the moment when the monster' became a decisively modern type of villain:

> Horror films before *Psycho* were essentially narratives that operated within the necessary limits that offered closure and security [...] *Psycho* sought to challenge this perspective by directly implicating the viewer in an amoral universe grounded in the psychic imperatives of its protagonists. (2000: 74)

Paul Meehan reiterates this view, recognising parallels between this type of psychological horror and film noir. Meehan observes that both genres act as 'studies in the psychopathology of evil' and 'revolv[e] around the pathology of psychotic individuals' (2011: 5–6). *Psycho* opened a decisively modern phase of horror cinema by focusing on the individual and transferring horror from the realm of the supernatural to the realm of the ordinary.

Return of the Repressed: Ordinary Evil in *Spoorloos*

The ordinary everyday man masking interior evil, modelled by Norman Bates, was succeeded by a first wave of Anglo-American 'slasher' villains, including *Halloween*'s Michael Myers (1979), *Friday the 13th*'s Jason Voorhees (1980), and *A Nightmare on Elm Street*'s Freddy Krueger (1984). 'Slasher' horror is a sub-genre of horror cinema that has generated some of the most commercially successful franchises and iconic villains. However, the motives of these bloodthirsty, machete-wielding villains often remain unclear.

Machete-wielding gore does not capture the more subtle emotions of dread and self-doubt characterising films like *Spoorloos*. Instead, Sluizer's film distances Lemorne from the bloodthirsty violence of these franchises and emphasises the bland ordinariness of his life and personality. For Kevin Wynter, its antagonist's bland or 'banal' nature is essential to understanding *Spoorloos*. Wynter describes *Spoorloos* as a type of film that 'manufactures a new intensity of "horror" not by accelerating the violence, but by decelerating the action and exposing viewers to the mundane activities of its killers and the very banality of the serial killer's approach to his crimes' (2017: 50).

The crime within *Spoorloos* is not a crime of passion. It is a premeditated experiment overseen by a calculated mind that turns each stage of preparation into a slow and almost monotonous process. The film gets under an audience's skin by showing the horrific possibilities lurking within the circumstances of ordinary life. However, the notion that a killer can have an ordinary presence and profile that escapes detection is not new. As Robert Confrath writes, 'part of the current mythology and disquieting role' that the serial killer plays in popular culture is 'because he is as likely to be a member of the company bowling team as he is an unemployed tool and die maker' (1994: 144). *Spoorloos* only exploits this trope, drawing out Lemorne's personality traits while emphasising his anonymity. In early sequences, Sluizer avoids shadowy imagery that would emphasise the mystery around Lemorne's motives.

Instead, he emphasises the small clues and signs that something is amiss with Lemorne's personality. An opening scene sketches out Lemorne's upper-middle-class status, showing an intimate look at his family life at his rural holiday home. This holiday home has particular symbolism within the film. It allows him to retreat from the outside world and conceal meticulous preparations for the abduction. However, the home also symbolises respectability. It acts as a veneer of success and class status, allowing him to avoid suspicion. Lemorne slinks without notice beneath the surface of his family and professional life.

On a practical level, the domestic settings of *Spoorloos* are at least partly due to independent film's budget restrictions, since smaller productions often feature less-expensive locations. On the other hand, the domesticity in *Spoorloos* has a specific purpose. It illuminates Lemorne's dual persona as a present father and husband, and as a duplicitous killer. Lemorne's behaviour is unnerving throughout the film. Only his family catch glimpses of small, easy-to-miss clues about his true nature. Immediately after Saskia's disappearance, the film flashbacks to the months preceding her abduction. This early sequence reveals significant red flags about Lemorne's character and shows how he conceals suspicious behaviour beneath the guise of normality. Lemorne sits with his wife and daughters in the garden of his rural home – the family exchange light-hearted conversation. The eldest daughter teases her parents about the house ('[T]his place is a dump') and her mother berates her jokingly in return ('Denise, you are unbelievable! If your grandma heard you!').

All is well and as expected within Lemorne's family. The members then sit down for a meal in their garden, and Lemorne picks up a bottle of wine to open for the table. He asks his youngest daughter, Gaby Lemorne, to open one of the table drawers for the corkscrew. Gaby opens the drawer and lets out a high-pitched scream. She finds that her father has planted a spider in the drawer, deliberately wanting to shock his daughter. Lemorne's wife, Simone, looks stunned, showing initial shock before Lemorne quickly turns the incident into a joke. He asks each woman at the table to scream to see who can make the most audible, high-pitched noise. The screams echo around the garden. The light-hearted tone of the gathering has soured, and a more ambivalent, sinister tone has darkened the family meal. Repeated incidents emphasise Lemorne's ongoing deception.

Figure 4. George Sluizer and the cast of Lemorne's family. (Credit to Jan Wich)

As a film that engages with ideas of human evil, *Spoorloos* seems suited to follow Wood's thesis for horror films that he described as the 'return of the repressed.' Within this formula, Lemorne's behaviour would represent the repressed desires that return as destructive and monstrous actions. Through villains like *Psycho*'s Norman Bates, monstrosity came to symbolise the return of repressed sexuality and 'otherness' suppressed through societal expectations to maintain the ideological status quo.

Wood characterises horror cinema as a mode based on the 'dramatisation of the dual concept the repressed/the Other [...] in the figure of the Monster' (2018b: 103). It certainly could be that Lemorne's behaviour is monstrous and unnerving because it enacts destructive desires that he repressed in adolescence. Under the 'return of the repressed' model, these desires escape Lemorne's subconscious at pivotal moments. For instance, when Lemorne picks his daughter up from school, he uses her to get into the car to rehearse how he can lock a victim in his car without suspicion.

Such telling moments seem haphazard and incidental. Even more notably, Lemorne's frequent disappearances to the holiday home arouse suspicions in his wife that he is having an affair. This confrontation between Lemorne and his wife, Simone, appears before Lemorne reveals his motives to Rex during their drawn-out car journey back to France. This scene functions as a sort of coded description of Lemorne's motives. As he describes to Simone, in an allusion that supposedly refers to the holiday home, but we know refers to his secret preparations,

> The house at St Come is like a passion. Because it's perfect, it's become a passion. You start with an idea in your head, and you take a step, then a second. Soon, you realize you're up to your neck in something intense, but that doesn't matter. You keep at it for the sheer pleasure of it. For the pure satisfaction it might give you.

Such deceptive behaviour is undoubtedly manipulative. However, it does not necessarily fit the template for the 'return of the repressed' that Wood and later critics have connected to diverse horror films. *Spoorloos* depicts a pattern of psychological manipulation in which Lemorne deftly deceives those closest to him. By the time Rex comes face to face with Lemorne in the final third of the film, we have already seen how *Spoorloos*' villain manipulates others' sense of reality. Lemorne's characterisation expands Wood's model of the 'return of the repressed' that critics have recognised within a diverse range of horror films.

With his duplicitous character, Lemorne does not directly fit the 'return of the repressed' model. Lemorne's distance from this template is clearer after a closer look at the thesis. In a review of Robin Wood's collected essays, David Greven writes that '[a]ll that society represses returns in frightening, monstrous form, a process the horror film perpetually enacts. Another way of putting it is Wood's succinct formula, "Normality is threatened by the monster"' (2019).

By contrast, Lemorne does not threaten normality. Instead, he personifies it. He personifies normality to such an extent that he evades detection and is near-immune from suspicion. So, how can we, as viewers, interpret *Spoorloos*? Is Wood's famous model of the 'return of the repressed' now redundant to an analysis of the film as a horror film? I argue not. Lemorne still echoes aspects of Norman Bates in *Psycho*, the film that Wood and others see as opening a modern phase of horror cinema.

Like the films that Wood analyses, Sluizer decisively focuses on the individual and prioritises the horror of the ordinary over the horror of the supernatural. *Spoorloos*' villain is an ordinary, everyman figure who still adopts characteristics of a particular type of antagonist: the serial killer. The following chapter discusses how this type of antagonist rose to prominence in a pivotal period for horror cinema. Lemorne captures the key traits identifiable across other films in the sub-genre of horror cinema that critics have identified as serial-killer cinema. In turn, this sub-genre overlaps with horror film conventions in highly recognisable ways that show *Spoorloos* as a distinct type of psychological horror film.

Chapter 3: A Portrait of a Serial Killer

'You start with an idea in your head, and you take a step, then a second. Soon, you realise you're up to your neck in something intense, but that doesn't matter. You keep at it for the sheer pleasure of it, for the satisfaction it might bring you.' These are Lemorne's words as he describes his obsession, which will lead to Saskia's abduction. However, many villains of late 1980s and 1990s cinema could have uttered these words.

The character type of the serial killer is that of an extreme and disturbing individual who develops an obsession with a violent fantasy. Regardless of his extremity, the killer is a cunning and deceitful individual, often capable of long-term, elaborate planning ahead of his actions. How we may interpret *Spoorloos* becomes more apparent when we realise that Sluizer's film was released on the cusp of a watershed cultural fixation with the threat and fear of the serial killer.

This moment saw serial-killer documentaries, true-crime drama and fiction flood into popular culture alongside box-office successes, including *American Psycho* (Mary Harron, 2000), *Seven* (David Fincher, 1995), and *The Silence of the Lambs* (Jonathan Demme, 1991). Serial killers have evolved into controversial figures of morbid curiosity within popular cinema. Serial killers seemed to symbolise something about the nature of random violence and how it can erupt out of nowhere to visit hapless victims at unexpected moments.

Expanding on the origins of the term 'serial killer' may be helpful before turning to its relevance to *Spoorloos*. Before the 1970s, at least in the United States, 'mass murderer' was the standard term and shorthand used by the US criminal justice system to refer to killers of multiple victims. The term 'serial killer' was conceived in the early 1970s by FBI veteran Robert Resseler. Resseler defined it as 'the unlawful killing of two or more victims by the same offender(s), in separate events,' with a cooling-off period between crimes of at least 72 hours (quoted in Bohn, 2014). This 'cooling-off period' (separating crimes over recognisable time periods) is crucial to cultural definitions of serial killing, as opposed to mass murder. The 'cooling-off period' was described by the psychologist Scott A. Bohn as 'one of the most important factors in defining the serial killer':

> Ted Bundy and the 'Killer Clown' John Wayne Gacy are good examples. They both slipped back into their seemingly normal lives in between their murders. That's where the cooling-off period comes into play – their ability to maintain an outward appearance of being completely normal and functioning in society and then, when the urge to kill becomes overwhelming, they strike again. (Bohn, 2014)

Bohn's words invite different responses. First, readers may perceive the clear link between fiction and true life that has characterised the serial killer from its early origins. Media coverage of real-life killers influences Bohn's understanding of the common patterns that structured the behaviour of serial criminals. The second important idea within Bohn's quotation is the concept of normality. The deceptive normality of the serial killer has become a recurrent feature of the character type.

Bohn understands the phenomenon of serial killing as a morbid subject of fascination. The serial killer is often represented in popular culture as a threatening 'Other' and dangerous outsider who reveals something about the dark side of human nature. The serial killer has a 'critical social function in defining conventional morality and behaviour by providing a ne plus ultra, against which normal society readily finds common ground' (Jenkins, 1994: 112). New representations of the serial killer are continually emerging in popular culture.

The influence of high-profile cases can be seen in the reception of contemporary true-crime dramas, including *Extremely Wicked, Shockingly Evil and Vile*, the Netflix drama starring Zac Efron as Ted Bundy. A 2019 review in *Vice* magazine argues that the Netflix programme 'makes Bundy the same archetype of attractive antihero that has always been available for a specific kind of (white) male lead' (Clark, 2019). Rather than depicting Bundy's crimes, *Extremely Wicked* focuses on Bundy's 'manipulative charisma and persistent claims of innocence' and neglects to examine the full consequences of his actions.

The story of Bundy still garners high publicity for *Netflix*. This profile seems to be because the juxtaposition between normality and horror within the serial killer fascinates audiences. There is no doubt that, as Philip Simpson puts it, the serial killer remains 'the ultimate alien outsider or enemy of society' (2000: 1). Two years before *Spoorloos*' release, Martin Scorsese was the executive producer for a similarly themed film, *Henry: Portrait of a Serial Killer* (1986). *Spoorloos* becomes more interesting in this context because it compares with representations of the serial killer as a cinematic villain. The serial killer was a character type that became increasingly prominent as a figure of morbid fascination in 1980s pop culture.

REPRESENTATIONS OF THE SERIAL KILLER IN POPULAR CULTURE

The serial killer is a figure of fear and panic that resonates across cultural boundaries in the US, Europe, and further afield. Serial-killer cinema is a genre that is closely linked to both psychological horror and detective or crime genres. *Henry: Portrait of a Serial Killer* was John McNaughton's controversial directorial debut, focusing on the true-life crimes of Henry Lee Lucas. Initially allocated an X rating from the Motion Picture Association of America, *Henry: Portrait of a Serial Killer* pushed the violence of the serial-killer film to the extreme. It depicted Henry and his roommate Otis pursuing victims through the slums of Chicago.

McNaughton's low-budget independent film, intended perhaps as a realistic look at our relationship to crime, violence, and media, received some similar responses to *Spoorloos*. Critics described *Henry: Portrait of a Serial Killer* as a 'relentless creepy study in evil' (Aldam, 2022). For Kevin Wynter, *Henry: Portrait of a Serial Killer* and *Spoorloos* are two pivotal films that capture the 'rise of the serial killer as a transnational figure of fascination in Western popular culture' (2017: 9).

The shape-shifting nature of the serial killer, as it changes across different cultural, political, and geographical contexts, also directs us to timely questions about horror. One school of thought maintains that the serial-killer film expands the familiar cat-and-mouse pursuit that structures supernatural horror, including vampire fiction. As Peter Hutchings observes, 'stressing the relative modernity of the serial killer should not obscure [the fact that] […] [m]ost horror monsters are in a sense serial killers. They kill a series of victims within particular narratives, and the more successful of them continue killing from one film to the next' (2004: 53).

However, other critics argue that the serial killer, as a character type, is linked to the commodification of violence in present-day popular culture. For Brian Jarvis, the serial killer is inseparable from a culture 'in which violent crime is marketed as a spectacle to be consumed' (2007: 326). Jarvis calls this effect the 'serial killer shock value.' He describes the appetite for true-crime drama and representations of serial killers as a 'profitable' market. The market 'both reflects and produces an apparently insatiable desire for images and stories of serial killing in a gothic hall of mirrors' (Jarvis, 2007: 328). This is the kind of market that transforms serial killing into a real-life and fictional spectacle.

A common criticism of detective or serial-killer fiction is that it minimises the real-life consequences of murder. Popular representations are accused of glamourising serial killers and turning them into calculating figures with the wit to outwit police forces. In *Spoorloos*, Sluizer seems aware of this risk and uses genre conventions to make a more muted commentary on the serial-killer phenomenon. The film makes the audience confront the drawn-out, absolute horror behind its villain's actions. The serial killer is a character who sees victims as specimens rather than humans. They see themselves at the top of a food chain engaged in an ongoing hunt for potential victims.

The world of *Spoorloos* is decisively modern, with motorway traffic, commercial travel, and tourism. The mingling of different groups and populations allows Lemorne to operate anonymously. Such settings are typical of films featuring serial killers. As Wynter observes, the serial killer reflects 'the violent contingencies of the modern world,' where individuals may easily disappear into a crowd, where they may conceal their activities behind the anonymity of cities, and they are mobile and able to cross regions, states, and borders undetected (2017: 59). This is a clear part of Lemorne's personality in *Spoorloos* as he blends in with modern environments. He abducts Saskia from a crowded, tourist-filled station on the freeway leading into France.

A glimpse beneath the surface-level normality of the serial killer is a pivotal part of *Spoorloos*. The appearance of normality defies efforts to understand patterns, and means we can never know who to trust and who to suspect. Each new suspect shows a new face of the serial killer. People keep 'buying' into characters, fascinated by an abnormality in the human psyche or patterns and behaviour that may be traced back to a recognisable motive. As Ashley M. Donnelly argues, 'In serial killer films, we know that the monster we are watching is supposed to look normal – we recognise this as one of the things which scare us. However, typically, his mask of normality slips, and we see him clearly for the monster he is' (2012: 21–2).

Spoorloos' screenplay explicitly acknowledges this aspect of Lemorne's approach to his grim and obsessive task. When he makes a first attempt to abduct an anonymous woman, he accidentally approaches his daughter's former volleyball instructor, who berates him for indiscreet efforts to pick up women. ('Take the highway in any direction [...] It's full of foreigners. Stop at any gas station, you'll find hundreds of women.') Within this crowded mise-en-scène, the camera has the ability to enhance claustrophobia. It uncomfortably lingers on faces in moments of emotional uncertainty. This camerawork emphasises *Spoorloos*' commitment to realism and finding eerie, unsettling terror in the minor details of everyday life.

Sluizer opens the film against the backdrop of the Tour de France, with the excitable radio announcer playing in the background of Rex and Saskia's arrival at the French gas station. The voiceover on the distant radio serves two purposes: first, it emphasises the anonymity of the gas station, with the commentary on the high-profile sport highlighting that action is happening elsewhere, whilst people pass through the gas station on their way to more important destinations. Second, this light-hearted atmosphere very quickly contrasts with the feeling that something is not quite right with an observer, the currently anonymous Lemorne, who watches the couple arrive from a distance. As Saskia walks to the station, sunlight is poking through as if reflecting her walking to the station with the sun in her eyes, unable to see clearly. The lens flares foreshadow deadly events, indicating that the characters cannot see what will happen to them. This segment is a stark sequence that sears itself into the audience's memory.

Typically, many audiences consume such films or shows that depict both real and fictional serial murders. But, to watch them, audiences need to forget or at least reduce the suffering of victims. They need to overlook, at least temporarily, the ethical consequences of such crimes. As forensic criminologist Xanthe Mallett observes, there is a clear risk of glossing over evil actions with unwarranted glamour. Mallett warns that

> The explosion of true crime in podcasts, streaming series, and books has fuelled our interest in violent and dangerous perpetrators and has increasingly meant the victims continue to be overlooked. Indeed, Ivan Milat, Ted Bundy, and Jeffrey Dahmer are household names. Yet Deborah Everist, Caryn Campbell, or Tony Hughes – victims of these violent killers, have been largely forgotten. (Mallett, 2022)

By contrast, this scene in *Spoorloos* and Sluizer's sequence framing spotlight Lemorne's victim. The muted violence of Lemorne's attack on Saskia is in contrast to the graphic and theatrical staging of an attack scene that audiences might see in a slasher film. The brief moment when Lemorne overpowers Saskia is a shocking moment. He lures her into his car with an offer of a gift for Rex and drugs her with chloroform while hidden from the view of passing travellers. As an audience, we may know the danger long before Saskia. However, until this moment of violence, the surface has remained overtly calm, relaxed, and neutral – almost maddingly so.

LEMORNE AS THE CALCULATED KILLER IN *SPOORLOOS*

Earlier in *Spoorloos*, Sluizer initially conceals Raymond's calculating motives beneath a shallow veneer of buffoonery. Without the audience knowing his long-term intentions, Raymond plans the logistics of the prospective abduction. What should be eerie and alarming becomes more unexpectedly light-hearted and slapstick. Sluizer shows us bird's-eye footage of Raymond alone in his holiday home garden. He rehearses lines to lure a stranger into his car. This scene collides with high-cadence synth music reminiscent of slapstick comedy. As he holds the car door ('What a coincidence! You may as well get in my car'), it falls out of his grasp and slams shut. Sluizer's delaying, understated tempo builds a sense of accumulative unease. This approach underpins *Spoorloos*' mode of horror.

This mode of horror is a decidedly psychological one. It offers a character study of a killer. We see the flawed human side of his psychology as well as his more able and cunning side. This approach resonates with Valdine Clemens' comments, in her study of Gothic horror, that the emergence of extreme violence within an unlikely character in horror is 'not simply to indulge in the wish fulfilment of unacceptable instinctual impulses, but to unlock such doors and to reveal a fuller view of human nature than is generally held' (1999: 39).

A further clue to interpreting *Spoorloos* within this framework comes after Lemorne approaches Rex, tracking him back to his flat in Amsterdam. Unable to resist Lemorne's offer, Rex grimly and wordlessly joins Lemorne in his car, which will travel from the Netherlands to France. Lemorne is not intimidated by the face-to-face encounter as they travel over the border. Lemorne mulls over his motives for abducting Saskia, which are rooted deep in his adolescence. Beneath the appearance of normality, Lemorne realises early in life that he is different from other people: 'When I was 16, I discovered something.' Lemorne's childhood recollections, told through flashback, include deciding to jump from the balcony of his home to prove he can perform dangerous feats, regardless of their risk or extremity.

In a flashback, a teenage Lemorne stands on the edge of a second-floor balcony, looking down onto the pavement below. He is daring himself to jump: 'Everyone has those thoughts, but no one ever jumps. I told myself: imagine you're jumping. Is it predestined that I won't? So, to go against what is predestined, one must jump. I jumped.' Despite breaking his 'left arm and [losing] two fingers,' Lemorne describes this moment as a 'holy event' and a life-changing realisation. In his mind, Lemorne was able to defy his own fate. Destiny seemed to tell him that he would not jump, and yet he still jumped. As a result, Lemorne convinces himself that he can defy destiny and commit acts that most people would be predestined never to commit. The sense of purpose that underpins Lemorne's mentality is unnerving.

As Lemorne continues, he explains how the idea for Saskia's abduction came from a pivotal moment in his adult life. During a family holiday with his wife and two daughters, they pass a child in danger of drowning in a rural canal. He jumps to rescue the child without a second thought. When his awe-struck daughter praises his heroism, he warns: 'Of course! I'm a hero. But never trust a hero. A hero is capable of rash gestures.' With his riddles and mysterious manner, Lemorne seems Sphinx-like. His motives are elusive, and the information he shares is incomplete and hinting at darker intentions.

However, if Rex is to find out what happened to Saskia, he must listen and ask Lemorne to explain his rationale. After hearing his daughter praise his heroism, Lemorne decides his good deed is worthless. He decides that 'her admiration wasn't worth anything' unless he proves himself 'absolutely incapable of doing anything evil,' the exact opposite. In other words, he is incapable of 'the most horrible deed that [he] could envision right at that moment.'

This type of scene is such a familiar cliché in detective fiction that it caused Roger Ebert, in a tongue-in-cheek quip, to name it 'The Talking Killer Syndrome' – 'in which the bad guys talk when they should be shooting':

> The villain wants to kill the hero. He has him cornered at gunpoint. All he has to do is pull the trigger. But he always talks first. He explains the hero's mistakes to him. Jeers. Laughs. And gives the hero time to think his way out of the situation, or be rescued by his buddy. (2013: 78)

Typically, in such films, this monologue leads to the calculating killer making a critical misstep, which allows the detective to locate and capture him. *Spoorloos*' narrative does not offer such closure. Typically, the detective takes a bird's-eye view of a case and marks a path to the killer. In *Spoorloos*, it is the killer who has the upper hand and who initiates a game of cat-and-mouse pursuit in a way that runs circles around his victim. Lemorne's desire to kill is not an uncontrollable appetite that leaves him open to capture but an intellectual exercise. He tells Rex that it was a short-term experiment to 'prove [himself] absolutely capable of doing anything evil.'

This scene touches on another aspect of serial-killer cinema: this type of cinema allows audiences to pathologise social violence. By 'pathologise,' we mean associate violence with individuals who have mental disorders. This process bypasses any role that social orders or hierarchies may play in the occurrence of violence. Myths about the 'serial killer' abound, and this often results in a distorted and pseudo-psychological focus on individual motivations. There is a cathartic side to this fascination. The serial killer is a singular and easily eliminated threat. Once the killer is eliminated, the equilibrium of a sense of safety is returned.

As some critics have said, 'attempt[s] to get inside the mind of a killer' reinforce the idea that violence is separate from structures and institutions in society (Hodgkinson, Prins, and Stuart-Bennett, 2017: 2). The solution in serial-killer cinema then becomes relatively simplistic. Without the serial killer, any underlying social problems or conditions go away. Philip Simpson argues that this distortion reinforces the social and cultural status quo. For Simpson, these serial-killer narratives redirect 'attention away from harmful economic and social policies, which do far more violence against persons than the relatively rare phenomenon of serial murder committed by isolated individuals' (2000: 19).

The serial killer, as the central antagonist, is brought to justice by the conclusion of these narratives. Audiences are reassured when social order is reinstated through the detective, the police, and law and order. The serial-killer narrative must be structured by easily recognisable patterns for this to happen. These patterns allow audiences to follow clues to the serial killer's motives and identity. Thus, serial-killer narratives typically end with a return to the status quo. The detective often uncovers motives behind the crimes. The narrative is usually structured by the victory of a representative of the law, and the thrill of the cat-and-mouse pursuit as the detective gets closer and closer to the killer. Over successive decades, this narrative structure has translated onto the cinema screen, with the archetype of Sam Spade (Humphrey Bogart) in *The Maltese Falcon* (John Huston, 1941) evolving into the private detective J.J. 'Jake' Gittes (Jack Nicholson) in *Chinatown* (Roman Polanski, 1974) and legal attorney Martin Vail (Richard Gere) in *Primal Fear* (Gregory Hoblit, 1996).

Spoorloos is the antithesis of this type of structure in serial-killer cinema. What happens when these sources of thrill and reassurance are undermined or overturned within the serial-killer narrative? *Spoorloos* seems to ask what unfolds when there is no reassuring representative of the law to intervene and halt the killer's actions. What happens if the serial killer is not apprehended and the status quo is not restored? If the killer remains free and able to repeat his disturbing acts, there is never a chance to avenge victims. *Spoorloos* provides an answer to these questions in its depiction of the actions of Raymond Lemorne.

THE DETECTIVE AND THE CRIMINAL: ROLE REVERSAL IN *SPOORLOOS*

The twist in *Spoorloos* combines contradictory traits within its antagonist so that Lemorne is both investigator and killer. Within detective fiction, the detective, or police investigator, is up against the clock to restore order and identify the killer before he strikes again. Raymond Chandler's famous private investigator, Philip Marlowe, anti-hero of *The Big Sleep* (1939) and *The Long Goodbye* (1953), captures the persona of the judicious, if flawed, detective. A drinker and a womaniser, Marlowe is the outsider with the perspective that allows him to decipher clues and interpret motives from minimal evidence.

In such detective or crime fiction, the less readers and audiences know about the victims, the better. For a detective to decipher a pattern across unfolding events, they cannot think about a victim alone and helpless. They must stay calm and rational, suppress feelings, and be able to assess potential motivations and courses of action. For critics like Charles J. Rzepka, there is a distinct narrative logic to such detective fiction that generates enjoyment as well as suspense. The detective novel encourages the 'exercise of our powers of imaginative invention.' It generates 'pleasure [...] in the sheer act of solving, or attempting to solve, the puzzle of detection' (Rzepka, 2005: 25). By the time the detective reveals the culprit or killer, 'the time we are allotted for solving the crime, as it were, will run out' (ibid.).

Detective fiction typically celebrates the victory of justice, and the audience identifies with a proactive detective who turns crimes into a game of deduction. *Spoorloos* contradicts this logic of detective narratives that viewers may find in more obvious box-office successes. By contrast, Lemorne is a killer who applies the cool calculation normally associated with the detective to his crimes. *Spoorloos* subverts conventional expectations of detective fiction. For Wynter, Lemorne has 'transposed the logic of the experiment from the laboratory to the streets of France' (2017: 55). The conventional detective narrative would conclude with the killer's capture. Instead, Lemorne becomes more confident in his capabilities as the film progresses.

Lemorne acknowledges and even embraces the 'sociopath' label, thinking that it distinguishes him from other people. Rex goes so far as to ask Lemorne whether he raped Saskia. Lemorne is perplexed by the accusation, almost disappointed that Rex would not realise that what he is capable of does not fit predictable sociopathic behaviour. This aspect of *Spoorloos* runs contrary to the logic of the serial-killer narratives that viewers may find in more obvious box-office successes. *Spoorloos* focuses on a killer who almost inadvertently becomes a serial killer. Lemorne sets out to see if he is capable of committing a profoundly evil act. Saskia is his primary and, at this point, sole victim, the pawn in a chilling and calculated experiment.

The rest of the story defies, to a great extent, the characteristics of the serial-killer genre that this chapter has already described. There is only a second victim because Rex is wrestling with what happened to Saskia and cannot reconcile himself to her disappearance. Three years after Saskia's disappearance, Lemorne only approaches Rex in response to appeals for information and to find out the lengths to which he is willing to go to satisfy his knowledge. This process reverses the standard narrative structure of the serial-killer genre because Rex is not in a position to decipher a pattern out of the turn of events that led to Saskia's disappearance.

The only way he can find out what happened to Saskia is to set aside his reasoning and calculations and do something entirely irrational – surrender himself to Lemorne's power. This is the opposite of the detective character type. As Mike D'Angelo points out, *Spoorloos* 'feature[s] an abrupt mid-film reveal that answers questions an ordinary thriller would have postponed for the climax' (2014). Unlike conventional detective films, Sluizer's film is structured to unnerve and discomfort its audiences. It reverses conventional feelings of satisfaction associated with detective fiction. This approach includes the victory of justice over evil and the enjoyment derived from procedural films.

Spoorloos is not about the calculation of the detective who eliminates the serial killer's potential motives and actions. Instead, as D'Angelo recognises, it is about curiosity – and an overriding 'need for closure – so overpowering that surrendering oneself to a madman seems like a reasonable price.' In interviews with Sluizer, this idea is made very clear:

> I'm trying to say in the film that perseverance can lead to obsession, and obsession can lead to worse – even murder. The film itself is trying to determine when a quality becomes a defect. Just like purity. My father said, 'Oh, if you are pure, that's good,'

when I was a little boy. Hitler also liked purity – so he killed everyone who wasn't pure. So, the film tries to balance itself between the plusses and the minuses of obsession. (Quoted in Glasby, 2016: 107)

For a detective to decipher a pattern, they cannot think about a victim alone and helpless. This approach is the opposite of what is seen throughout *Spoorloos* in scenes after Saskia's kidnapping, where Lemorne consolidates his control over unfolding events. Some three years after Saskia's original disappearance, he observes Rex from afar, discovering that he can goad Rex into more desperate actions – actions that will culminate in the dramatic finale.

Rex is not being rational, and he cannot distance himself from the crime to discover who Saskia's abductor is. *Spoorloos* denies the audience the reassurance gained through the presence of a credible and reliable detective. In addition, we must also consider that Lemorne, instead, adopts the traits that we may generally identify with detectives. Lemorne is a killer who applies the cool calculation generally associated with the detective to his crimes. Midway through the car journey into France with Rex, Lemorne conveys the impression that he is somewhat bored with his life and always looking for new and extreme intellectual stimulation. Lemorne offers to reveal Saskia's fate but with a perverse condition, the requirement that Rex relive what she endured in her final moments: 'I'll tell you. I promised you that. But the only way to tell you, is to make you share the exact same experience.' We also hear Lemorne hint about the circumstances of Saskia's demise when a traffic warden stops the car that Rex and Lemorne are travelling in. Asked why he isn't wearing a seatbelt, Lemorne produces a medical exemption certificate. If he inflicted on Saskia the 'most horrible deed' that he could think of, we get a clear hint in this scene: 'I'm a claustrophobe.'

As Lemorne talks, his monologue only confirms how trapped and woven Rex is within Lemorne's plotting and conspiracy. Not only can Lemorne divert all efforts to link him back to the scene of Saskia's abduction, he can also frame his encounter with Saskia as a sickly, pseudo-supernatural moment. A predestined moment that brought Saskia into his orbit, almost as if a deity or fate willed her death at Lemorne's hand. Lemorne, as we are reminded through flashback, was a hair-width away from choosing another victim. When another young woman is willing to get into Lemorne's car (under the guise of helping him attach a trailer to the back of it), Lemorne is about to drug her with chloroform. However, before he can do so, he sneezes into the drugged handkerchief and is forced to retreat before he collapses. This turning point precedes Lemorne finding another victim. Rex's hands are tied, and he cannot escape danger. As Lemorne slyly observes, 'Destiny, Mr Hofman.'

It would be overly easy, from a brief survey of these unusual sequences, to dismiss *Spoorloos* as too dark and nihilistic. The presentation of Lemorne's actions and their repercussions places *Spoorloos* squarely within wider debates about genre and taste within horror. The shape-shifting nature of the serial killer, as it changes across different types of cinema, also directs us to timely questions about horror and about how horror has changed over time. Before the year of *Spoorloos*' release, perceptions of evil and monstrosity were informed by a first wave of 'slasher' franchises. These include *Halloween* (1979), *Friday the 13th* (1980), and *A Nightmare on Elm Street* (1984). In contrast to these adrenaline-fuelled films, Spoorloos is more concerned with the malleability of the human psyche. It is concerned with Raymond projecting an image of respectability.

The Silence of the Lambs (1991) is the closest film to embody this persona most acutely. Hannibal Lecter is not treated as a monster in a classical sense. He is white, probably heterosexual, intelligent, and had a liberal profession. He may be a cannibal, but he is highly urbane and sophisticated. This appearance of normality defies efforts to understand patterns and means we can never know who to trust and who to suspect. As within *The Silence of the Lambs*, crime within *Spoorloos* is not a crime of passion. It is a premeditated experiment overseen by a calm and calculating mind.

The Silence of the Lambs' approach to its subject echoes what Carol Clover has critiqued as the moderating of slasher cinema and attuning it to milder tastes. Clover describes it as coming 'awfully close to being slasher films for yuppies – well-made, well-acted, and well-conceived versions of the familiar story of a female victim-hero' pursued by a villain of superior capabilities (1992: 20) Clover argues that these films affirm the vanity of their villains, treating them as objects of glamourous fascination.

Spoorloos could not be critiqued in the same way. *Spoorloos*' more unpredictable narrative structure is far from cold or indifferent to violence. The violence in *Spoorloos* is a game for Lemorne and exists for his absurd conviction that he can defy fate and destiny. However, *Spoorloos* is not only a 'talking killer' film, to echo Roger Ebert. It is also a film that has generated much talk and debate about its balance between horror and psychology. Much of this talk, echoing Clover's comments, has focused on genre boundaries. This debate questions whether *Spoorloos* is a thriller or a horror and how the terror in *Spoorloos* is interwoven into a narrative that addresses the loss experienced by its central protagonist, Rex.

Again and again, critics argue that an unusual type of horror is at work in *Spoorloos*. Les Roberts recognises this type of horror as deliberately disorientating even whilst presenting ordinary life and locations. While Roberts describes *Spoorloos* as a 'near-forensic examination of a moment of violence,' he also identifies the 'sense of irresolution and absence that engulfs Rex and drives his dark quest for knowledge' (Roberts, 2014: 19). While depicting the calculating sociopathy of a serial killer, *Spoorloos*' horror also contrasts this villain with Rex's desperate, disturbed psychological state. As he continues to search for Saskia, he becomes more reckless and psychologically vulnerable. He takes on debt to fund media appeals to the public. His obsession causes his new girlfriend to leave him, and he experiences flashbacks to the day of Saskia's disappearance, becoming susceptible to panic attacks.

However, despite its main villain's forensic attention to detail, *Spoorloos* embraces the Gothic mode and tradition. The final scene of Rex buried alive underground, gasping for air and flailing around in the underground darkness as his sanity finally crumbles, is unmistakeably Gothic. The disturbingly theatrical staging of Rex's fate is a Gothic spectacle of excess, while Lemorne is the Gothic villain who defies all moral limits and restraints. This ending chimes with Fred Botting's description of the Gothic's 'fascination with transgression and the anxiety over cultural limits and boundaries,' which 'produce[s] ambivalent emotions and meanings in [its] tales of darkness, desire and power' (1996: 2).

The serial-killer narrative has decisively Gothic origins. As Philip L. Simpson observes, most modern thrillers and horrors 'portray their killers as modernized Gothic villains – shadow seducers who simultaneously live on the margins of society and within it. They stalk victims, mostly women, through a dark mythic landscape teeming with supernatural portents' (2000: 35). *Spoorloos* draws on this Gothic heritage in memorable ways. Lemorne is an agent of death who defies the boundaries between reality and the dark imagination. Lemorne's own twisted, individual psyche is projected onto the outside world. His behaviour sucks both Saskia and Rex into a scenario that Lemorne has orchestrated, a perverse hall of mirrors with only fatal choices at the end. The following chapter addresses these Gothic aspects of *Spoorloos* in more detail. It looks at this Gothic side of Sluizer's film in terms of its villain and its depiction of grief and obsession within Rex, Lemorne's second victim after Saskia.

Chapter 4: Grief and the Gothic in *Spoorloos*

Whilst *Spoorloos* focuses on the horrific consequences of Lemorne's actions, its horror also stems from depicting and meditating on the painful effects of grief and loss. Recent film scholarship has demonstrated a revived interest in this theme within horror films. In a 2021 article, 'Horror Films and Grief,' Becky Millar and Jonny Lee argue that the 'use of antagonistic forces in horror – what we broadly refer to as "monsters" – is effective at representing the disruption to one's core, taken-for-granted beliefs or "assumptive world" that is characteristic of grief' (2021: 171).

Indeed, other commentaries argue that grief is central to horror cinema and that the generic violence of horror reflects the emotional rupture of grief. The screenwriter Stephen Sheil captures this sentiment well when he says that

> Death is transformative; for those left behind, the experience of grief and loss opens up another world. It's a world where the violence of death is not just an ever-present possibility, it's an inevitability. And there's no telling where or when it might strike – it's unmindful, implacable, remorseless. It's every unkillable Michael Myers or Jason Voorhees – and there's always a sequel. The landscape of grief is one that is haunted by this specter; it's always there lurking, ready to strike. (2016)

The characteristics of these types of monsters – whether knife-wielding, Michael-Myers-style villains or more subtle villains like Lemorne – allude to specific aspects of the emotional disruptions caused by grief. The narrative trajectories of these horror films trace the protagonist's efforts to overcome and defeat the monster.

As Millar and Lee's article states, 'by establishing the intimate connection between the protagonist's grief and the presence of the monster in their life, horror films about grief institute a narrative association between the resolution of the protagonist's emotional need and the resolution of the protagonist's struggle with the monster' (2021: 175). *Spoorloos* subverts this narrative association by depicting Rex as unable to resolve his emotional needs. Also, the only way for Rex to resolve his emotional need is to place himself in the hands of the monster. *Spoorloos* is about the paralysing effects of grief, and the final shot of Rex entombed alive underground symbolises how grief can swallow up all of life's potential and growth.

This symbolism is most acute in the final scene, but the theme echoes across earlier parts of the film. Consider the scene in which Rex chooses to respond to an anonymous postcard from Lemorne. Rex sits in the forecourt of the Café Beaux des Amis, brooding and silent next to his new girlfriend, Lieneke, who reluctantly indulges Rex's continuing obsession. On the surface, Rex is sensitive and even paranoid: 'He's watching me. I can feel it.' Lieneke can only respond to this bleak frame of mind with exasperation, telling Rex that 'he's playing with you. He's followed the story through the papers and wants to see how far you'll go.' Rex's justifications for responding to the taunting postcards are seemingly irrational. He goes so far as to reveal that he is 'afraid' that Lemorne will 'stop sending the postcards' and that he'll 'never know.'

Figure 5. Rex and his new girlfriend, Lieneke, argue about Saskia. (Credit to Anouk Sluizer)

Ironically, at this point when Rex's motivations are most doubtful, Sluizer's camerawork makes the audience acutely aware of Lemorne's observant presence. Lemorne watches the fraught conversation between Rex and Lieneke from a distance. Lemorne is positioned in the background of the shot. He slides into the chair at the adjoining table in Rex's eyeline as Lieneke dissuades him from pursuing further leads on Saskia. The shot reveals how Lemorne has deftly immersed himself in Rex's world. He is capable of isolating Rex from any remaining support and is slowly and corrosively chipping away at Rex's sanity. This frustration continues despite Rex never knowing what Lemorne even looks like.

The History of the Gothic

This type of narrative does not necessarily make *Spoorloos* a Gothic film. The Gothic label has been applied to a diverse range of films and media. Here, it is useful to offer a brief history of the Gothic and its shape-shifting status across diverse national cultures. The Gothic is a wide-ranging mode of literature and entertainment that dates back centuries and requires further definition. Horace Walpole's *The Castle of Otranto* (1765) is celebrated as the first Gothic novel and the forefather of the modern Gothic. Featuring a tyrannical father, lord of the eponymous castle, visiting cruelty upon his wife and family, the novel's second edition called it 'A Gothic Story' (1982: 3–106).

Walpole's subtitle originally intended to combine terror with a haunted, medieval aesthetic. However, beyond early texts like *The Castle*, the Gothic rapidly emerged as a broad, sweeping frame of reference for the bizarre and extreme. The Gothic mode includes hauntings, strange dreams, and apparitions. It features passionate, destructive emotions that unfold against a medieval, disorientating background of claustrophobic castles and ruins.

Such Gothic imagery became the stuff of nightmares and a highly fashionable mode of fiction. This Gothic mode began with Walpole and encompassed the work of authors such as Ann Radcliffe, Walter Scott, and Edgar Allan Poe. The fear of being buried alive is a prominent fear in Gothic horror. It is a form of death that Poe famously described as 'the most terrific of [the] extremes which has ever fallen to the lot of mere mortality' (2015: 497). Poe is the author of some of the most memorable Gothic stories that feature premature burial, including 'The Fall of the House of Usher' (1839) and 'The Premature Burial' (1844).

Andrew Mangham writes that, throughout the nineteenth century, 'live burial was paradigmatic of unexpected movements and unwelcome forms of understanding. The idea of being buried alive emerged as a ghastly emblem of knowing – truly knowing – what it was to be beleaguered, victimised, and terrified' (2010: 10). Gothic stories of live burial are terrifying and provoke feelings of powerlessness and desperation. Lemorne recognises the dread that such a fate provokes. He says in a discussion with Rex during their car journey, 'And as black cannot exist without white, I logically conceived the most horrible deed that I could envision right at that moment. But I want you to know, for me killing is not the worst thing.'

Spoorloos' final scene is decidedly Gothic as Lemorne entombs Rex in the ground and seals his terrifying anonymous death. However, beyond this final scene, *Spoorloos* explores the dark side of human psychology in a way that can also be traced back to early Gothic writers, including Poe. For Poe, Gothic horror is not solely in period castles and dark graveyards. The actual threat to the human mind lies in its neuroses and fears. In Poe's 'The Black Cat,' his narrator famously states that 'perverseness is one of the primitive impulses of the human heart – one of the indivisible primary faculties, or sentiments, which give direction to the character of Man. Who has not, a hundred times, found himself committing a vile or a silly action, for no other reason than because he knows he should not' (2007).

Poe's short story 'The Imp of the Perverse' (1845) similarly follows a man who, like Rex, is a victim of his self-destructive impulses. After having poisoned a man with a toxic type of candle – thereby leaving no evidence of his crime – the story's narrator describes living off the estate of the victim. However, despite getting away with his crime, he is sabotaged by a self-destructive impulse to confess, describing this urge as one seeming to be almost willed on by the ghost of his victim. Walking down the street without suspicion, the narrator describes an irresistible desire to confess his crime. 'And now,' he says, 'my own casual self-suggestion that I might possibly be fool enough to confess the murder of which I had been guilty, confronted me, as if the very ghost of him whom I had murdered – and beckoned me on to death' (Poe, 2022). He eventually yells out his crime to a crowd in the street before his arrest.

This Gothic type of self-destructive impulse is recognisable in the obsessive side of both Lemorne and Rex. The imp of the perverse infects both Lemorne and Rex in the film – Lemorne describes being unable to resist the urge to prove his evil capabilities, and Rex cannot resist the urge to discover Saskia's fate even at the cost of his own life. A Gothic mind twists and perverts the world around it, transforming its surroundings to reflect its own dark desires or anxious fears.

More recent critics have understood these psychological themes and sought to understand and define the Gothic more broadly. They frequently see it as a genre of opposites. Catherine Spooner captures the ubiquitous character of the Gothic as it continues to evolve in 'contemporary Western culture.' Spooner writes that the 'Gothic lurks in all sorts of unexpected corners. Like a malevolent virus, Gothic narratives have escaped the confines of literature and spread across disciplinary boundaries to infect all kinds of media' (2007: 8). Through the broadening of definitions, the Gothic has experienced revival after revival across multiple decades. In their 2021 study *Contemporary Gothic and Horror Film*, Keith McDonald and Wayne Johnson also offer a valuable description of the tensions within the Gothic. They write that the Gothic is a mode that focuses on 'light versus dark, order versus disorder, nature versus supernature, reason versus superstition' (2021: 1).

McDonald and Johnson also provide further insight into the Gothic's adaptability. They write that Gothic horror addresses 'two key impulses: the consequence of the pursuit of knowledge and the seeking of consolation.' Citing examples of twenty-first-century horror, McDonald and Johnson observe that horror 'provides answers to grief (*The Babadook*, 2014), guilt (*The Ritual*, 2017), and the nature of sin (*Tumbbad*, 2018)' (2021: 2).

This Gothic interpretation of grief is also present in *Spoorloos*, especially in the eerie symbolism of the golden egg. In Saskia's dream, she 'float[s] all alone through space, forever,' trapped in 'unbearable' loneliness within the shell of a golden egg, which she cannot escape. The golden egg haunts Rex's memories of Saskia and comes to symbolise his loss. The original Dutch-language title of Krabbé's novella (*Het Gouden Ei*), the golden egg is an ominous object. It is a sign of the uncanny and a foreshadowing of Rex's fate. It is an ambiguous symbol that, as Sabine Vanacker observes, has very literal and grisly meanings:

the egg is not an image of fertility but its opposite, an image of death, annihilation, of a becoming into nothing. At a certain level, creation coincides with destruction, with the loss of identity, the destruction of existence by means of flux. (1995: 103)

Throughout the film, the symbolism of the golden egg becomes darker and more threatening, underpinning a narrative of loss. In her dream, Saskia describes another golden egg flying through space, threatening to collide with her own egg. The image of the two golden eggs colliding in the dream is an eerie visual counterpart to Rex's and Saskia's shared fates at the film's end. Saskia's disappearance leaves her – at least in Rex's mind – stuck in limbo, forever moving through space and trapped without any closure or revelation. In later scenes, Rex is haunted by recurring nightmares about 'the golden egg' that Saskia imagined herself entrapped within. In the film's closing moments, bright light fills the screen. Rex gasps for air in his entombed coffin, which echoes the shape of the titular golden egg and fulfils the dark promise of Saskia's dream.

THE GOLDEN EGG IN *SPOORLOOS*

The golden egg foreshadows Saskia's fate and Rex's fate in the film's final scenes. The egg also represents Rex's feelings throughout the film. Saskia's absence overshadows the film, yet she is also frozen in time. She exists in Rex's memory as a still image. This is the image that Rex cannot forget and that he continues to obsess over in subsequent years. This emotion is reflected in specific scenes within *Spoorloos*. At a key moment, straight after Saskia has left, Rex takes a photo of the bicycles on the car. This photograph is poignant, with a last trace of Saskia's red hair in the distance, and also a symbolic, telling piece of evidence. Rex is later convinced that the photo shows her speaking to her abductor, frustratingly just out of shot. He will repeatedly return to this image. Rex becomes an increasingly pathetic, melancholy figure who is doomed to revisit the same moment again and again.

This type of experience has a particular type of expression in the Gothic. In particular, it draws *Spoorloos* into a type of Gothic that is labelled by critics, including Diana Wallace and Andrew Smith, as 'the Female Gothic' and 'the Women's Gothic' (2009: 1). Ironically, *Spoorloos* taps into this type of Female Gothic since it features two male protagonists. This Gothic mode typically depicts female protagonists navigating hostile landscapes that embody the risks and dangers of patriarchal culture. Wallace and Smith see the origins of this genre in the earliest Gothic texts in the late eighteenth century, including those of Ann Radcliffe. The female protagonist who must navigate disorientating landscapes is an archetypal character. 'It is Radcliffe's novels,' they write, 'with their heroines in flight from male tyrants across fantastical landscapes and in search of lost mothers entombed in womb-like dungeons beneath patriarchal castles which we now tend to characterise as the beginnings of "Female Gothic"' (2009: 2).

The Female Gothic has evolved into a more distinct form of psychological horror, in which women find themselves wrangling with the psychology of family relationships and repressive domestic environments. In an essay on Shirley Jackson's fiction, Roberta Rubenstein describes the Female Gothic as a mode that emerges from the domestic novel. The Female Gothic contains stories of paranoia and murder, and the archetypal scenario where a wife is convinced a husband is attempting to murder her. Such a genre is a stage and 'battleground in the struggle for autonomy' in the face of 'stifling expectations placed on women' (Rubenstein, 1996: 309).

On first reading, *Spoorloos* seems far away from this domestic territory. This may be especially true since the film's central dynamic focuses on two male characters. However, the film's complexity lies in the unusual blurring together of reason and unreason. The obsessive paranoia that critics have identified with the Female Gothic is evoked at unexpected moments. In a way, this might be unsurprising. Gothic narratives often use opposites to generate tension – masculine and feminine, light and dark, good and evil.

Yet, *Spoorloos* defies these boundaries, and this blurring of contrasts is crucial for its storytelling. *Spoorloos* draws its male protagonist into the emotional realm of the Female Gothic, exposing him to issues of vulnerability and mortality. This narrative technique weaves a complex web between on-screen characters and off-screen viewers, broadening the emotional spectrum beyond the crudely gendered terms of the Female Gothic.

GENDER ROLES AND THE FEMALE GOTHIC IN *SPOORLOOS*

Steven Jay Schneider and Kevin Sweeney, in their essay titled 'Genre Bending and Gender Bonding: Masculinity and Repression in Dutch "Thriller" Cinema,' were the first to recognise the distinctive gender politics within *Spoorloos*. In their close reading of *Spoorloos*, Schneider and Sweeney recognise the film as a compelling example of Dutch thriller cinema. In this genre of thriller film, *Spoorloos*' 'love story' between Rex and Saskia has relatively straightforward psychoanalytical connotations (Schneider and Sweeney, 2005: 180). From the film's start, Schneider and Sweeney argue that Rex, as a heterosexual man, is insecure in his relationship with Saskia. The gulf between the couple is apparent in the symbolism of Saskia's dream about the golden egg. The nightmare is about being engulfed by an overwhelming loneliness – a feeling that we may deduce she feels in her relationship with Rex. Tension between Rex and Saskia becomes even more apparent in the following scene.

As Saskia finishes narrating her dream, the car abruptly runs out of petrol. The vehicle is trapped in the tunnel and invisible to oncoming traffic. The headlights of approaching cars form the shape of golden eggs. The couple becomes frustrated with the car's loss of power and begins to argue back and forth. Rex is exasperated by Saskia's heightened panic about her nightmare ('This is no time to talk about dreams!'). Saskia's claustrophobia causes her to panic as she searches for a flashlight on the car's backseat. Rex loses patience and decides to walk out of the tunnel and back to find gas at a station they passed earlier on the road. Saskia panics further, screaming at Rex and begging him not to leave her alone in the darkness ('Rex, don't leave me here alone!'). Sluizer frames Saskia's panicked movement in the car, her face distorting into tears and distress. He enhances the claustrophobia of the scene. Instead of disturbing the shot with a loud noise to create a jump scare, Sluizer amplifies the sound of the traffic, which initially drowns out the sound in the car. The sound then dims and fades up again with the sound of Saskia sobbing as she begs Rex: 'You can't leave me here alone!'

Figure 6. Saskia is left alone in the car. (Credit to Anouk Sluizer)

For Schneider, this moment in *Spoorloos* foreshadows the gulf that will come between Rex and Saskia. This moment will play out again and again in Rex's head. Haunting moments in *Spoorloos* – disquieting memories, Lemorne's taunting postcards – threaten Rex's conscious mind. He follows clues promising to expose the motives behind Saskia's disappearance. Even his new girlfriend, Lieneke, who reluctantly indulges Rex's continuing obsession, cannot get through to him: 'Saskia is gone, Rex! She's gone!'

However, in response to these images of obsessive recall, Schneider has a surprising interpretation. He only sees a persistent denial that comes from guilt. This guilt arises from homoerotic desire. The Dutch thriller, he writes, displays an 'underlying thematic preoccupation' with repressed obsession or, specifically, a male protagonist's 'anxiety about […] a female partner, anxiety that generates an imaginative and obsessive desire for control that winds up being repressed' at the film's conclusion (2005: 182).

Schneider and Sweeney identify a homoerotic tension between Rex and Lemorne. The obsession that Rex experiences is akin to a man in love. He is waiting for postcards full of broken promises and desperate for a face-to-face rendezvous. Suppose Lemorne is 'the masculine initiator.' In that case, Schneider and Sweeney write that Rex 'adopts a traditional "feminine" position relative to Lemorne, one that is analogous to Saskia's position relative to Rex earlier in the film' (2005: 196).

The final twist of the film is a chilling metaphor for repressed sexuality. Rex is trapped 'not so much in a coffin as in the closet' (ibid.). A perverse twist of fate, 'the freedom [Lemorne] initially grants Rex from normative (monogamous and lifelong) heterosexual commitment' is something he cannot fully enjoy due to guilt and denial of his sexuality. Entombed for eternity beneath the earth with Saskia, he is frozen in time next to the girlfriend he subconsciously wishes to escape.

While gesturing towards *Spoorloos*' nuanced gender politics, feminist critics, who are well-used to analysing images of women within popular cinema, may be sceptical of how this reading simply overlooks Saskia as its female protagonist and sole female victim. However, *Spoorloos* deftly transplants elements of the Female Gothic onto a series of power games that subvert gender expectations. The Female Gothic typically focuses on a heroine or woman vulnerable to the whims of a traditionally violent Gothic male. *Spoorloos*, by contrast, focuses on its male protagonist's mental state. Until the final scene, it is almost as if Saskia's disappearance becomes a backstory to the film.

Spoorloos depicts the disintegration of Rex's peace of mind in the aftermath of Saskia's disappearance. Roberts concludes that the horror of *Spoorloos* ensues from 'the violence inflicted on Rex's sense of being-in-the-world that grows and grows throughout the film' (2014: 55). Three years after the disappearance, Rex's determination to find out what happened to his girlfriend has not waned. He appeals for information and funds a media campaign to raise the profile of Saskia's disappearance. His obsessive devotion catches Lemorne's eye, and Lemorne observes Rex from afar before seeking out contact with him. Rex continues putting up posters around the area with her photograph. Lemorne's interest is piqued. As he says to an acquaintance whilst passing one of these posters, 'I admire his perseverance.'

Sluizer uses this scene to emphasise again how Lemorne's true self is concealed in plain sight. This scene gives Lemorne further dialogue, which deliberately deceives his companion: '[Y]ou wanted to crucify anyone who kidnapped young girls. I even asked: "What if I'd done it?" You laughed in my face!' Cross-cutting scenes, which flit back and forth between Lemorne's deceptive life and Rex's search, generate suspense as the contrast between the two becomes more explicit and more transparent. This contrast is apparent when Lemorne invites Rex to chosen locations close to Saskia's disappearance. These include the Café Beaux des Amis beneath the balcony of Lemorne's flat. He sits at an adjacent table to Rex and Lieneke, closely listening to them argue about Rex's relentless pursuit of the truth. Rex is so near to the source of his misery and yet so far.

This panning shot in the café seems to foreshadow later events in *Spoorloos*. It shows that Rex is brushing against the risk of a dangerous encounter with Lemorne. In this case, the shot appears to foreshadow later events of the film, suggesting that Rex is heading into a dangerous situation. The meditative camerawork in this shot differs from faster-paced earlier sequences. It presents a slow panning shot that gradually reveals Lemorne's uncomfortable proximity to Rex. This approach allows the audience to study the characters' expressions and process subtler on-screen emotions. The scene captures the unnerving limbo that Rex finds himself in. He is trapped in a specific life phase, unable to process Saskia's loss and move on due to his struggle with his memory of her.

Ironically, his loss means Rex is unable to recognise more obvious, growing threats to his own life in the form of Lemorne and his close observation of Rex's obsessive concern for Saskia. Rex's obsessive grief is the catalyst for the events that follow, with Lemorne taking advantage of Rex's fragile state. By grappling with conflicting emotions of grief and obsession, *Spoorloos* – despite its outward framing as a thriller – does appear to interact significantly with the typical melodrama of the Gothic. Melodramas contain 'pathos, overwrought emotion, non-classical narrative structure, sensationalism, and moral polarity' (Cagle, 2016: 142).

Indeed, melodrama and Gothic horror have been categorised as overlapping modes of film in film scholarship. Linda Williams is perhaps one of the earliest critics to argue at length that melodrama and horror are primarily physical or 'bodily genres' which foreground 'screams of fear in horror, sobs of anguish in melodrama' (1999: 270). Melodrama is also a prominent feature of the Female Gothic and had its most acute manifestation in a cycle of 1940s films recognised as the 'paranoid woman's film of the 1940s.'

Mark Jancovich describes these films as 'obsessive or paranoid' due to the 'pervading sense of threat that these women experience, usually from a husband or lover' (2007: 3). These films include Hitchcock's *Rebecca* (1940), Robert Siodmak's *The Spiral Staircase* (1946), and Max Ophuls's *Caught* (1949). Such films often combined thrills with Gothic romance, conventional Gothic settings, and an alluring, if mysterious, romantic lead. Hitchcock's *Rebecca*, described as launching the paranoid woman's film, captures these traits with the foreboding house of Manderley and the brooding Max de Winter.

A significant body of critical scholarship has interpreted these films as a cultural expression of uncertain gender relations in the period after the Second World War. Marjorie Rosen describes such films of female psychological turmoil as valorising women who are 'pleasantly pliable and even appealingly incompetent.' Rosen argues that these films base narratives on a 'quietly masterful creature recognising no limitations to her own endurance' (1975: 205). However, later critics have suggested that such readings are limiting and do not recognise how the genre evolved after the immediate post-war period. By the end of the 1940s, Jancovich writes that 'these films were increasingly disassociating themselves from notions of Gothic horror and identifying themselves with hardboiled crime fiction' (2007: 4).

The woman-in-peril premise did not quite chime with lesser-known films, including *The Snake-Pit* (1947), which began to depart from the 'Gothic fantasy world of literature and history' and reflect more tough, realistic settings (ibid.). The extreme, emotional behaviour of the imperilled female protagonist evolved into the need for a more aware hero or heroine who must learn about perception and be able to see and interpret the most minor signs. These were a 'larger cycle of films, at least as concerned with masculinity as femininity' (ibid.: 15).

Richard Armstrong offers the most straightforward take on the traits of these 'woman's films' and, notably, their connection to horror. Armstrong writes that

> Part of what is uncanny about certain films is the excess of emotion. While melodrama pervades the horror scenario, a kind of horror materialises when melodrama becomes excessively emotional. *The Haunting*, *The Innocents* and *Carnival of Souls* […] all dealt with a woman's loneliness before the prospect of eternity. (2012: 24)

The 'mourning film' that Armstrong describes here retreats from sensationalised depictions of violence. Instead, such films are attuned to the aftermath of a painful event and the processing of grief. Mourning is often conveyed through a disjointed approach to time. These films use cinematic flashbacks and ellipses that blur the lines between memory and reality and between the past and the present. The films are frequently slow-moving and meditative. The disorientated protagonists of these films are also passive and restrained.

The use of cinematic devices (slow motion, still and lingering images, and long-shot sequences) deliberately manipulates the realism and trustworthiness of the cinematic image. A viewer will feel that a threat hovers at the edge of sight. As Armstrong writes, the image in the mourning film 'teeter[s] on the fringes of an ontology, simultaneously calling into question the veracity of what we see, while making it apparent that "something" is present' (2012: 40).

Mourning and Grief in *Spoorloos*

Spoorloos combines Gothic themes with the formal traits of this type of 'mourning film.' It differs from the focus of other mourning films by focusing on a grieving man rather than a troubled or paranoid woman. However, *Spoorloos* is a film attuned to grief. Horror cinema is already widely recognised as a genre that grapples with loss and grief. Hauntings and separations often emerge as recurrent motifs within horror. As Stacey Ann Baran writes, with reference to films including *The Exorcist* (1973), *Don't Look Now* (1973), and *The Changeling* (1980), horror films 'typically address the loss of a loved one and what terrors may lurk as the family, spouse, parents, or otherwise find themselves literally or metaphorically haunted by the trauma of their past' (Baran, 2023: 3).

Spoorloos uses 'the golden egg' as a recurrent motif for grief. The imagery of the golden egg often erupts into unanticipated scenes. The golden egg is a haunting symbol of the pervasive nature of grief and how different ways of reconciling oneself – denial, work, new beginnings – can be hopeless. This type of haunting is prominent in *Spoorloos*. In the opening scene where Saskia recounts her dream, she states, 'This time there was another golden egg flying through space. And if it were to collide, it'd all be over.' This dream is referenced throughout the film and haunts Rex's final memories of Saskia. Rex will revisit this conversation in future years. He semi-understands that they are a premonition of Saskia's fate, which neither he nor the audience can fully understand before the finale. This imagery suggests a blurring of the past and present and conveys the persistent nature of Rex's grief-induced obsession with Saskia. This ambiguity echoes the 'scenarios of separation, of separation and return, or threatened separation' that Mary Ann Doane associates with the woman's film of the 1940s (1987: 73).

Saskia's highly cryptic dream prefigures the traumatic rupture in Rex's life after her disappearance. In a later sequence, three years after Saskia's disappearance, we see Rex begin to hallucinate visions of Saskia. He has been persuaded to visit 'Anduze, Bois Vieux' by Lieneke, his new girlfriend, in the same Gard department of southern France where Saskia vanished. Rex is walking with Lieneke along an isolated country track and recalling the similar roads he travelled along during the final holiday with Saskia. He imagines his holiday car, complete with bicycles strapped to the roof, passing them by on the curb. The sequence flashbacks to the inside of the car, depicting Saskia and Rex on their car journey. They sing along to radio songs and practise French vocabulary under the holiday sun. Returning to the present, Rex collapses near the roadside, lost in a fatigued trance as he repeats, again and again: 'Golden egg. Golden egg. Golden egg.'

Sluizer uses this device of the ellipsis to move forward and backwards between Rex's past and present. This motion enhances the feeling of absence that permeates the film. This unpredictable editing suggests a dislocation within Rex's mind and memory. It also enhances the audience's sense that, despite trying to navigate unfolding events, Rex's death has already been decided by fate or destiny. The titular golden egg traps Saskia within the open, unreachable abyss of outer space. It is also a recurrent, unavoidable symbol that foreshadows her own death and Rex's demise. The shape haunts Rex's memory, and the looping narratives will allude back and forth to the golden egg as the central image. In the early sequence where Rex leaves Saskia in the tunnel's pitch-black darkness, he returns to find that Saskia has left the car and is waiting at the entrance, dazed and visibly afraid.

In an evocative long shot made into a promotional poster for the film, Sluizer frames Saskia in a glaring cloud of light in the shape of the golden egg. This image transforms her into a far-away, ephemeral figure, foreshadowing her eventual disappearance. In the final shot, when Rex awakes inside the coffin, his only source of fading light is a lighter that forms and fades into the egg shape. The last image that seers itself onto Rex's vision is the shape of the golden egg. This egg seems to symbolise the inevitability of Rex's fate. Its recurrent imagery, as it haunts Rex's memories and dreams, alludes to the closed coffin that will be Rex's final grave. As discussed earlier in this chapter, the idea of predestination is prominent across *Spoorloos*. Rex's final line of dialogue, spoken after he drinks the drugged coffee that Lemorne has offered him, perversely echoes Lemorne's earlier reflections: 'I told myself: "Imagine you're drinking. Where is it predestined, I won't drink? So, to go against what is predestined, I must drink."'

What makes *Spoorloos* so horrifying is not solely Rex's loss but also the film's exploration of the finality of death. The Gothic themes in *Spoorloos* manipulate and play with this fear of finality. The film's story is more about the futility of avoiding the finality of death. This theme of destiny echoes throughout *Spoorloos*. The 'unconquerable force' of destiny is a prominent theme in the Gothic tradition. Dani Cavallaro describes the obscure boundary between choice and destiny as a theme that originates with Poe. A Poe protagonist, such as the narrator of his famous narrative poem 'The Raven' (1845), 'masochistically pursues' knowledge, asking 'increasingly unanswerable questions of his ominous visitor out of a perverse desire to be denied acceptable explanations for his abysmal sorrow' (Cavallaro, 2002: 11).

The perverse twists and turns of destiny structure the narrative of *Spoorloos*. Even in earlier sequences of the film, there are hints of this theme, as if Saskia and Rex's fate at the hands of Lemorne is somehow inevitable. After the couple leaves the tunnel, they weigh up which station to stop at on their journey. They pass an earlier gas station and decide to push on to get further along their journey before stopping for drinks and a break. This is the station at which Saskia disappears. In Wynter's reading, *Spoorloos*' twist ending is a memorable expression of this cold nihilism. That is, 'the attempt to gain meaning' or understand the motive of Saskia's abduction 'leaves Rex buried alive in a coffin, in the very abyss of the curiosity that once possessed him' (Wynter, 2017: 59).

Yet even before this final scene, Rex finds himself trapped within a shape-shifting and strange landscape. His inability to resist Lemorne's invitation echoes Doane's description of the Female Gothic as 'adventure stories with passive protagonists' (1987: 185). Despite his helpless position in *Spoorloos* and its central mystery, Rex is forced to question everything around him and look for hidden meanings. After Lemorne makes initial contact via mysterious postcards, Rex must try to decipher ominous signs and grapple with puzzles that Lemorne uses to provoke him. The film's narrative structure is organised by emotion that Tarja Laine calls a 'hopeless hope.' This 'hopeless hope' allows 'spectators to participate in the protagonist's project – and will them to succeed, overcome, and triumph – while they know [it] to be hopeless from the beginning' (Laine, 2011: 28).

Laine identifies a shift in thrillers during the 1980s and 1990s away from the conventional suspense of Hitchcock-style thrillers. Conventional thrillers rely on audience identification with heroic characters, as seen in iconic Hitchcock thrillers including *North by Northwest* (1959). By contrast, late twentieth-century thrillers are more existential and often place antagonists or unsympathetic protagonists in the spotlight. These films deliberately place the audience in a dilemma. They may be uncomfortable with the unethical character on screen, yet the film is structured so that viewers identify with this character's actions and perspective. The juxtaposition of perspectives is essential to *Spoorloos*.

Throughout the film, we may wonder how we are supposed to feel in response to the events on screen. This is a prominent theme in incidental moments within the film. An awareness of media and how it can be manipulated echoes throughout the film: the camera which Rex uses to take the final photograph of Saskia, the media campaign that Rex launches (which persuades Lemorne to get in touch with him), and the computer which Rex uses to print posters about Saskia's disappearance. We find it distressingly inept in the face of the reality of Saskia's disappearance – despite its ubiquitous nature and scope to reach multiple audiences, it is the avenue which allows Lemorne to reach Rex.

Laine's conception of 'hopeless hope' also reflects the symbolism of the golden egg within *Spoorloos*. Laine interprets the golden egg as reflecting 'the obsessive spiral Rex has leapt into, which keeps him captive, as in a gravitational field' (2011: 33). Due to Saskia's disappearance, Rex is trapped in a specific life phase and unable to process her loss and move on due to his struggle with his obsession. Ironically, his loss and issues mean Rex is unable to recognise more obvious, growing threats to his own life in the form of Lemorne.

There is a slow, conscious building of dread through Sluizer's unnerving close-ups of Rex's blank face. The discordant music, scored by Dutch composer Henny Vrienten, is designed to disorientate the viewer. By contrast, *Spoorloos* has a more formally bleak sense of pathos, evoking a sense of hopelessness distinct from formal horror conventions. In Laine's phrasing, '[t]his has two consequences. First, it denies Rex any possibility of free will, and second, all hope for a preferable outcome is rendered hopeless. It is this notion that organizes the whole narrative structure of the film' (ibid.). In Rex's case, his experiences imply an imposing sense of melancholy.

This melancholia comes through Rex's ongoing dialogue with Lieneke, his new girlfriend, who is increasingly exasperated by his behaviour. We learn that Rex receives numerous letters about potential sightings of Saskia following his media appeal. One letter claims she is 'working in a brothel in Marseilles' and another, from a psychic, predicts that Rex will see her shortly in an unexpected place. Rex is plagued by an obsession that he cannot move past or process. This frustration is visually expressed when Lieneke resolves to leave Rex after realising that he will never be able to forget Saskia. She leaves Rex's flat with sad parting words that recognise the exasperating situation: 'If there'd been no Saskia. But there was and is a Saskia.'

Rex is left alone, and when he turns to look at his computer, he sees Saskia's name appearing and reappearing on the monitor screen. The name forms different patterns across the screen, moving in different directions as Rex watches, almost resigned to what he sees. He knows he is imagining what he sees on the screen and cannot look away from the subject of his obsession. The presentation of such scenes contrasts with conventional narrative tropes, which resolve all loose ends and disputed plot points by the end of a narrative.

Rex's psychological condition echoes Freud's psychoanalytical concept of melancholia. This idea distinguishes 'grief' from 'mourning.' Grief is a raw, easily led emotion that is vulnerable to anger and self-destruction. By contrast, mourning is an active process of working through grief to accept and reconcile oneself finally to loss. Freud's essay 'Mourning and Melancholia' (1917) describes the person who suffers from melancholia as an enigma who is caught in limbo by being unable to face and reconcile themselves to loss. He writes that 'the inhibition of the melancholic seems puzzling to us because we cannot see what it is that is absorbing him so entirely' (Freud, 2001: 245–6).

While the mourning person never entirely loses their sense of their person, the loss itself absorbs the melancholic person. 'The melancholic,' Freud elaborates, 'displays something else besides which is lacking in mourning – an extraordinary diminution in his self-regard, an impoverishment of his ego on a grand scale' (ibid.: 246). Such a description chimes with Rex's ordeal in *Spoorloos*. His experience of grief is never punctuated or resolved by any cathartic realisation of the extent or consequences of Saskia's disappearance. Symbolically, it is only in the final scene, when it is too late to do anything else, that Rex screams and cries out Saskia's name again and again.

Melancholia and Place in *Spoorloos*

Repressed grief is characteristic of Rex's persona throughout *Spoorloos*. We never see him scream until the final moments. As Baran writes, the 'cathartic scream' is essential to various types of horror. It 'functions as a purging or exorcism' and 'as a narrative device wherein its actualization demarcates the act of conquering grief, typically at the climax of the film, and of liberating oneself' (Baran, 2023: 2). This lack of catharsis traps Rex in his melancholy obsession and leaves him vulnerable to Lemorne. Even before meeting Lemorne, Rex is living in an in-between world, a space between the living and the dead. His eventual fate is a manifestation of this living death. As Les Roberts states, his death is a 'space of transition, the claustrophobic interior of the coffin becomes an inescapable liminal landscape: a space in-between the worlds of the living and the dead' (2014: 16).

This representation of time and space is central to the Gothic. Spaces are meandering within Gothic fiction and often contain allusions to other threats and dangers. Gothic tropes include 'doppelgängers, mirror images, and abysmal symbols with the Gothic aesthetic of terror. These tropes range from hauntingly enigmatic landscapes to claustrophobic interior spaces that are both terrifying and attractive' (Drizou, 2016: 126). Such enigma is apparent in *Spoorloos*' physically transitory settings: the gas station, the freeway, and the border between France and the Netherlands. All these locations are transitory and busy, yet at the same time empty. Place has a peculiar meaning in *Spoorloos*. Andrews describes these locations as adapting the famous phrase of the French anthropologist Marc Augé, 'a non-place' (1995: 107). A non-place is a distinctly modern type of location – an airport lounge, a motorway, or freeway – that is characterised by indifference and anonymity. This non-place is 'emptied and contingent,' stripped of any of the 'slow accretion of memory and identity' that come with places invested in by community and community practices.

The locations in *Spoorloos* reflect an 'existential limbo' that plagues Rex. *Spoorloos* is set far away from stereotypical Gothic settings and does not feature a supernatural plot twist. Yet, as the primary location of Saskia's disappearance, the service station is the perfect setting for a story of physical and psychic loss and disorientation. When Rex and Saskia first arrive at the station, the cheerful, unrelenting murmur and motion of people and traffic are indifferent to the personal circumstances of visitors.

As Les Roberts writes, this is a place empty of memory or security: 'emptied and contingent sociality engages the slow accretion of memory and identity. Time is measured in other people's comings and goings' (2014: 54). Think of how often we see Rex in such transitory spaces that are 'empty of memory.' These ordinary, everyday settings, described by Roberts as a 'restless geography of transit,' (2014: 19) facilitate Saskia's disappearance. When Saskia and Rex first arrive at the gas station, the endless motion of travellers, tourists, and vehicles has a light-hearted, transitory pulse that can so quickly transform into an anonymity indifferent to loss and danger.

When Saskia leaves Rex to go into the gas station (and never returns), the realisation of her disappearance slowly dawns on Rex. An extended four-minute sequence becomes increasingly panicked and claustrophobic. Rex takes a photo of the car laden with bicycles as a memento of the trip. Impatient for Saskia's return, he strolls into the crowd-filled station to check in but does not see her. Still, uncertainty is yet to set in. He wanders back outside, and only when he realises Saskia is nowhere to be seen does he begin to wonder. He sits alone, and concern begins to set in. He leaves a panicked note on the car bonnet. His panic worsens, and he barges through the forecourt, shouting Saskia's name.

As the camera follows Rex into every room and corner, we see the bright and breezy spaces of the gas station in a new way. The station becomes a labyrinthine hall of mirrors where Rex catches sight of women resembling Saskia, only to be disappointed. Saskia has become part of the crowd and never reappeared. These spaces include the gas-station forecourt where Saskia first disappears, the square where Raymond lures him through postcards, and the cross-border journey back to France. Ironically, one scene in particular disrupts this near-seamless flow of anonymous locations. Rex and Raymond stop at a well-known site near the French freeway as a rest stop on their journey. *Mémorial pour l'Avenir*, or the Memorial for the Future, commemorates a multiple-vehicle crash, the second deadliest road traffic collision in France's history (B.L., 2013).

The allusion to commemorating a public tragedy is ironic. The choice of location almost deliberately contrasts with the anonymity of Saskia's fate. This site is salt in the wound – an apparent reference to unresolved grief within Rex and the extent to which Raymond will probe at this pain. This potent juxtaposition of the memorial and other more anonymous spaces heightens the sense of cruelty within the film. Saskia's fate is anonymous whilst others are commemorated.

After the camera shows Rex entombed below ground, the scene shows Raymond sitting in the garden of his rural holiday home, presumably the site where he buried both Saskia and Rex. The eerie transition between Rex's screams and Raymond's tranquil evening, sitting above the very ground where the couple's bodies lie, symbolises Lemorne's mastery of destiny that he sought to achieve throughout the film. As Kevin Wynter observes,

> It is important to note that Raymond does not bury Rex and Saskia in a vacant lot or in some distant woods far from the comings and goings of his everyday life. He instead buries them beneath his vacation home, where he can remain in proximity to the bodies of his victims and the achievement of his crime. (2017: 54)

Spoorloos begins with a violent separation and ends with a violent reunion of sorts. In its beginning lies its end: the disappearance of Saskia sows the seeds of Rex's own destruction. The darkest aspect of grief is the absence. Like a person who has lost a limb, they half feel as if the limb is still there before they realise that it is truly gone. Rex is forced to realise, again and again, that Saskia is absent.

The fragmentary nature of *Spoorloos* shows that memories and grief are not chronological. They are a pool of recollections, impressions, and acute emotions that can erupt into your life at any moment. When an object of love is removed, all that remains is a memory of them and the slowly fading personal details. This stark manifestation of the unexplored grief is at the heart of the film. After their long, cross-border journey, Rex and Lemorne return to the gas station where Saskia first disappeared. Lemorne produces a flask of drugged coffee and issues his ultimatum: '[But] the only way to tell you [what happened to Saskia], is to make you share the exact same experience.' When Rex tries to seek confirmation that Saskia is dead, Lemorne refuses a definitive answer. 'Drink,' he repeats, 'I drugged her and now I'm going to drug you. [...] After, you'll experience exactly what she did.' Rex initially turns away from Raymond in disgust. He then makes his way to the spot where he last saw Saskia – a once-shaded spot under a tree where he and Saskia buried two sets of coins, promising to love each other forever.

This pang of his final memory of Saskia overwhelms Rex. He wrestles with himself, pacing back and forth, increasingly frantic and eventually despairing. Raymond watches dispassionately from the car. The music amplifies and heightens the tension. We don't know until the last minute whether he will drink. In an abrupt moment, he sprints back to the car – and he drinks.

Before the film's ending, Rex offers a grimly ironic final line that explains his choice and echoes Raymond's earlier line: 'I told myself, "Imagine you're drinking". Where is it predestined I won't drink? So, to go against what is predestined, I must drink.' Ultimately, the horror at the centre of *Spoorloos* is not just Rex's and Saskia's fates.

The horror also ensues from the way that Raymond annihilates all traces of his victims and their memories, experiences, and identities. Perversely, it is here that Rex and Saskia are reunited in their original love, as the film's final shot is a tracking shot to a newspaper headline reporting Rex's disappearance.

When Rex reencounters the coins, he realises that he is clutching at a part of Saskia that he can never regain. And it is this feeling of loss and yet nearness which explains how the film ends. The past interrupts the present in a way that predicts the future. In the same way, the future intrudes upon the present at the beginning of the film within the premonition in Saskia's dream of the golden egg. Focusing on grief and sociopathic pathology, *Spoorloos* gets under the skin of its audience through a brutal and stark examination of grief and loss.

With this exploration of grief, *Spoorloos* echoes and foreshadows an emerging field of contemporary independent horror. This type of independent horror combines an emphasis on grief and loss with an art-cinema tone and restraint. Critics have offered a range of alternative labels, including 'post-horror' and 'elevated horror,' that have provoked ongoing debate. The title of this category of film is especially controversial. David Church, in one of the first monographs dedicated to this generation of horror, writes that such films favour 'minimalism over maximalism. They largely eschew jump scares, frenetic editing, and energetic and handheld cinematography in favour of cold and distanced shot framing. They have longer-than-average shot durations, slow camera movements, and stately narrative pacing' (2021: 11).

Such films are repeatedly seen as a 'new breed' of early twenty-first-century horror associated with prominent production companies, including A24 (Rose, 2017). However, *Spoorloos* reflects and foreshadows the priorities of these post-horror films by focusing more on the long-term, destructive consequences of grief and mourning than on overt horror. The following chapter takes an alternative look at *Spoorloos*. As Church argues, 'some critics have posited post-horror as a "new genre" or "new subgenre" of horror cinema.' In contrast to this assumption, the distinct qualities of post-horror are apparent in earlier periods of cinema. Church writes that 'post-horror should be 'far more accurately described as an aesthetically linked cycle within the longer tradition of art-horror cinema' (2021: 3).

Spoorloos echoes the formal traits of this type of post-horror cinema. Except for its closing scene, *Spoorloos* has the visual markers of realism rather than of horror cinema. Its primary register is unease, suspense, and dread rather than gore, violence, and disgust. The following chapter analyses how *Spoorloos* foreshadows the existential ethos of post-horror cinema that emerged decades after the millennium. Grief is the catalyst for horror in *Spoorloos*, and the chapter's discussion will tease out how this premise connects the film to a broader tradition of art-house horror that, in modern-day commentary, is called 'post-horror' or 'elevated horror.'

Chapter 5: *Spoorloos* as Post-horror Cinema

'Post-horror' has been a significant topic in horror cinema discussions since the early 2000s, gaining particular attention with a release of art-house horror during the 2010s. While traditional horror often revolves around supernatural threats, post-horror narratives tend to delve into psychological conflict and distress. The term was first coined by Steve Rose in the *Guardian* to describe a new wave of horror that was seeping into mainstream cinema, replacing jump scares with a more existential dread (2017).

The label 'post-horror' has quickly gained prominence in popular culture since 2017. The Barbican, for instance, hosted a film screening series in the summer of 2022 titled 'Post-Horror Summer Nights' with films including *It Follows* (2014), *The Witch* (2016), and *Hereditary* (2018) (Rose, 2022). Film critics widely critiqued the term, and Rose eventually published a rebuttal, also in the *Guardian*, stating that 'Whatever your feelings about the label post-horror, we can surely agree something extraordinary was happening in cinema in the mid-2010s. In addition to the movies above, the years 2014 to 2018 also gave us *It Follows*, *The Babadook*, *Raw*, *Split*, *A Girl Walks Home Alone at Night*, *Under the Shadow*, *Green Room*, *A Quiet Place* and Jordan Peele's phenomenal *Get Out*' (Rose, 2022).

At first glance, it may seem unusual to discuss *Spoorloos* in the context of a seemingly contemporary trend in post-millennial horror cinema. However, David Church, in one of the earliest book-length studies of post-horror cinema, argues that 'one of the major characteristics of such films is their sustained thematic exploration of what Silvan Tomkins terms "negative affects" (including grief, sadness, shame, anger). These affects connect post-horror cinema to themes in "serious" arthouse dramas' (Church, 2021: 13).

Church's description certainly resonates with *Spoorloos*. This resonance is despite the release of Sluizer's film 20 years before 'post-horror' became a prominent term in film circles. *Spoorloos*' shape-shifting tone decentres familiar horror tropes – jump scares, supernatural entities – through the formal techniques of art house cinema, allowing characters and spectators to soak in emotionally fraught moods of anger, guilt, and obsession. By encouraging its audience to identify with its protagonist's grief, *Spoorloos* refuses to provide any expected genre experiences that many may anticipate in horror cinema. Instead, it echoes the techniques and adaptability of art house cinema.

The purpose of this chapter is twofold. First, it draws out certain stylistic traits in *Spoorloos* that identify it as part of this international horror tradition labelled 'post-horror.' Second, it will demonstrate that this mode of cinema, labelled 'post-horror,' is not a new phenomenon. *Spoorloos* is a convincing example of a horror film that captures horror's ongoing relationship with psychological themes that certain critics interpret as a new development. *Spoorloos* emerges as one of the horror genre's most unlikely meditations on loss and grief. It captures a form of social and psychological horror that is receiving renewed attention in the 2010s but is not unprecedented in the genre.

In 2017, Steve Rose described a tendency in recent films to depart from 'well-established themes' in horror, including 'supernatural possession, haunted houses, psychos, zombies.' Instead, these films offer a more subtle, exploratory look at 'big metaphysical questions' and universal experiences (Rose, 2017). While nominally marketed as horror cinema, films such as *It Comes at Night* (2014), *The Witch* (2015), and *A Ghost Story* (2016) avoid the spectacle and visual conventions associated with horror cinema and, instead, spotlight the more existentialist experiences of their main characters.

In *A Ghost Story*, for instance, a man who is killed in a car crash haunts the home of the 'grief-stricken young widow' who cannot see him. When she moves out, he is forced to remain there in spirit form. Time passes, and new occupants move in. Years later, the building is demolished, yet his spirit still endures. As Rose writes, 'time loops in on itself, and the story expands from personal *trauma* into the realms of cosmic speculation' (2017). This strand of more meditative horror has particular relevance for contemporary horror film.

In present-day film circles, there are growing efforts to name and critique an emergent cycle of twenty-first-century films which draw together conventions from art-house and horror cinema. Labels including 'slow-horror,' 'prestige-horror,' and 'elevated-horror' have been stamped on recent films by Robert Eggers (*The Witch*, 2015), Ari

Aster (*Hereditary*, 2017; *Midsommar*, 2018), and Jordan Peele (*Get Out*, 2014). These are films which Jacob Trussell describes as a 'crop of emotionally complex horror distancing itself from popular popcorn-infused terror,' showing the genre to be 'far more nuanced than [the public] ever gave it credit for' (Trussell, 2018). Some critics have heralded such post-horror films as a new dawn and 'golden age' for horror cinema. They write that if horror is unfamiliar, it is generic territory for adult fears and emotions (Zinoman, 2018). Such films are praised for avoiding jump scares and more common scare tactics with a tendency towards more understated and realistic storytelling.

Beyond Post-horror Cinema

However, this chapter argues that these 'post-horror' films are far more accurately described as one part of a decades-long, evolving cycle of art-house horror cinema. This cycle has consistently wrestled with psychological issues. This chapter is not the first piece of writing to articulate this critique. Adam Lowenstein most ably expresses this view when he describes elevated horror as 'still ensnared in unresolved issues from criticism on 1970s horror, especially the distinction between social and psychological horror' (2022: 296). Lowenstein outlines elevated horror as less a genre in its own right than a long-term, evolving form of cinema that is characterised by a 'refusal to separate the social from the psychological' (ibid.).

Lowenstein dismisses the claim that the 2010s have welcomed a more 'elevated' or grown-up form of horror. Instead, he writes that horror across different decades frequently places personal lives, anxieties, and contradictions within a broader, more threatening context of plagues, monsters, and violence. Horror filmmaking has constantly challenged classical Hollywood cinema with psychologically complex characters, social commentary, and shock-driven narratives. The genre's power was recognised in the 1960s and '70s with the rise of filmmakers including John Carpenter, Wes Craven, David Cronenberg, Brian De Palma, Tobe Hooper, and George A. Romero.

By recognising this tradition, it becomes clear that genre cinema is less of a genre than an umbrella encompassing a range of stylistic characteristics and tropes. That is, as Lowenstein writes, 'what we can trace in the trajectory between the 1970s and the 2010s is not a genre in ascension or decline but rather a genre always already committed to acting its age. No matter its era of origin and against all conventional expectations, horror knows how to age well' (2022: 310).

Spoorloos is a horror film that echoes the logic of Lowenstein's argument. His commentary recognises that terms such as 'post-horror' echo a long-term tendency amongst horror-sceptic film critics to denigrate horror cinema. These critics often praise films that conjure subtle, haunting 'atmosphere' as the seeming antithesis of spectacle and gore associated with the genre. Church articulates qualms around the reception of contemporary horror. He states that 'the monster conjured in the high-minded viewer's imagination has often held critical precedence over blatant images of the abject, with "psychological horror" seen as a more refined and restrained aesthetic that is more at home in the art house than the grindhouse' (Church, 2021: 9).

Early reviews of *Spoorloos* echo these descriptions of post-horror and repeatedly emphasise the film's more understated thriller elements over the ending's horror. 'Poetic,' 'appalling,' and 'memorable' are just some of the descriptions *Spoorloos* garnered immediately after its release (Wells, 2020; Meares, 2021; Nayman, 2018). As discussed in the introduction to this book, critics offered repeated comparisons with Hitchcock. Such comparisons often conceal their assumption that genre labels, including horror, are too unsophisticated and low-brow to address Sluizer's film.

However, *Spoorloos* was broadly welcomed by critics, who praised the film's 'appalling, horrific climax' and the artful construction and elegance of the film's cryptic narrative (Wilmington, 1990). Rather than confronting the spectators with excessive or gleeful gore, *Spoorloos* is more effective at exploring the destructive consequences of obsession. By contrast, Todd McGowan sees *Spoorloos* as stripping away seductive 'movie magic' and presenting the audience with an unflinching look at the 'unsolvable and irredeemable' nature of trauma: 'When we see Rex […] buried alive in the horrific final scene of *The Vanishing* and are in a sense buried with him as Sluizer films inside the coffin, we experience the trauma of an inescapable and terminal confinement' (2011: 223–4).

However, whilst these critics retreat from calling *Spoorloos* a horror film, this chapter argues that the film broadens our understanding of horror cinema. *Spoorloos* shows that there can be divergent cinematic strategies for generating sensations of horror, dread, suspense, and other emotions. Although Spoorloos has a visceral shock ending, much of the film's duration focuses on how Rex mourns Saskia's disappearance. Loss and grief, especially of a loved one or intimate family member, is a prominent theme in post-horror cinema. These experiences take the shape of a potentially imagined monster or threat. Rather than being explicitly supernatural, these threats are implied to be potential figments of a traumatised imagination, with the threats symbolising unresolved grief and mourning.

In his book *The Pleasures of Horror*, the critic Matthew Hills describes explicitly this kind of effect within horror. Hills writes that horror is not solely about unnerving stimuli or monsters. He cleverly intervenes in horror studies when he argues that such films do not need to be 'event-based' but can be 'entity-based' viewing experiences. An 'entity-based experience' relies upon elements of the cinematography and mise-en-scène. These elements include low-level lighting, low-resolution images, and static within sound design. They can generate an ambience that could be interpreted as horror or generate an anticipation of horror (Hills, 2005: 26). Hills describes this effect in scholarly language. He argues that innovative films, including *The Blair Witch Project* (Daniel Myrick and Eduardo Sánchez, 1999), are often defined by an 'objectual indeterminacy' (ibid.). *The Blair Witch Project* 'allows for cognitive evaluations that the Witch exists and is a threatening force, but it also withholds confirmation of the Witch as a fully or clearly defined object' (ibid.).

SPOORLOOS, POST-HORROR AND DUTCH CINEMA

Spoorloos has few conspicuous quirks. However, if, as Hills argues, affect precedes events, horror can ensue from diffuse and ambiguous sensations that cannot be linked to specific threats or characters. In *Spoorloos*, Lemorne is a decidedly tangible and real-world threat. However, the editing and structure of the film also play with time. This anticipates the conventions that would become associated with post-horror cinema. Sluizer's directing and use of recurring imagery enhance the audience's sense that, despite trying to find out the cause of past events, Rex's death is already predestined – thus creating the 'hopeless hope' effect that this book discussed in Chapter Four. Rex's dilemma in *Spoorloos* is based on psychological ambiguity rather than explicit, visceral violence. As Rex explains to his new girlfriend, 'Sometimes, I imagine that [Saskia's] alive somewhere far away. That she's very happy and so on. Then I have a choice. Either I let her go on living and never know anything, or I let her die and find out everything.'

Sluizer aims not merely to shock his audience but to compel them to engage with the film's themes in more detail. The audience's active involvement in understanding and interpreting the film's themes is crucial. *Spoorloos* centres on Rex's behaviour and life, which almost adopts an 'uncanny' effect because, in his grief, he is not mentally living on the same plane as everyone else. Instead, he is living a parallel, un-dead life as Saskia continues to haunt him.

Critics have studied these themes within *Spoorloos*. Many of the formal traits that critics, including Church, identify with the attributes of post-horror also echo the formal techniques that some commentators have identified within a specific national strand of Dutch cinema. In the years after its release, *Spoorloos*' initial success was framed by a particular set of expectations around the style and content of Dutch cinema. The conventions of this strand of Dutch cinema are less well known than cinema from neighbouring European countries.

Ernest Mathijs' edited collection *The Cinema of the Low Countries* (2004) offers a more sustained effort to define familiar tropes within Dutch cinema. Mathijs recognises that Dutch cinema, or cinema of the Low Countries, is less well known than other regional or national cinemas. However, he also identifies some characteristics that point towards the emergence of a 'cinema of cultural relevance,' a trend to which *Spoorloos* significantly contributes. Low Countries cinema often features 'a quest into identity crises – gradually revealing that we can no longer trust what we see or hear, reality becoming a dream':

> Minute details in language, visuals and behaviour cast doubts on the truthfulness of the authentic settings in which characters live and travel, until we finally give up looking for truth and settle, with the characters, for quiet contemplation – death, lunacy or a surrender to strangeness. (Mathijs, 2004: 10)

This strange and macabre ethos contrasts with the visceral gore that has characterised other types of art-house cinema in Europe. *Spoorloos* was released at the end of a decade in which European film was attaining a global reputation for combining horror and realism and depicting explicit transgressive violence and explicit sexuality. In the 1970s and 1980s, filmmakers from France (including Jean Rollin), Italy (Lamberto Bava), and Spain (Bruno Mattei) were broadening the controversial themes of modern horror cinema. In a collection dedicated to European cinema, Steven Jay Schneider associates a 'more graphic, sensational and transgressive type of European horror cinema' with the 'opening up of the restraints' within the European commercial film industry (Schneider, 2007: xx).

This international brand of 'Euro-horror' became synonymous with gore and excess. The most notable example of this tendency is within 'New French Extremity' cinema. Stylistically diverse and yet preoccupied with graphic sex and violence, titles from this movement include *Twentynine Palms* (Bruno Dumont, 2003), *Trouble Every Day* (Clare Denis, 2001), *Irreversible* (Gasper Noe, 2002), and *Baise-Moi* (Virginie Despentes and Coralie Trinh Thi, 2000). These films left a decisive mark on European film culture. New French Extremity cinema's legacy is famously described – and derided – by James Quandt as 'determined to break every taboo' by introducing 'images and subjects once the provenance of splatter films, exploitation flicks, and porn' into the 'high-environs' of a French national cinema which is more traditionally associated with the filmography of artistic, iconic auteurs (2004).

By contrast, Dutch cinema has a more understated approach to gore and terror. It is more attuned to the 'surreal melancholy of everyday life.' As Mathijs states, Dutch thrillers tend to question the reality of their protagonists' lives. This observation echoes Sluizer's own description of *Spoorloos*. According to Sluizer, the film reflects what we 'see in daily life, exaggerated, seen through a magnifying glass, all the evil in the film can be seen every day. It's not a documentary but neither is it invention' (Tunney, 1990: 81). Sluizer ranks lingering dread over direct gore and jump scares. As noted in the introduction to this book, this tone foreshadows the work of the Austrian director Michael Haneke. Haneke is a director who prioritises realism, presents violence in an observational manner which emphasises how it may erupt out of random events, and offers minimal narrative resolution or closure. Tanya Horeck and Tina Kendall, in their edited collection *The New Extremism in Cinema: From France to Europe* (2011), associate Haneke with a controversial cinematic trend in Europe called 'New Extremism.'

Without 'down[playing] the differences in style, approach and intent' between national contexts, Horeck and Kendall argue that European horror offers an 'uncompromising and highly self-reflexive appeal to the spectator that marks out the specificity of these films' (2013: 1). Offering their inclusive label of 'New Extremism,' covering films from Spain, Germany, Belgium, and other European countries, they identify a common focus on heightened moments of tension which do not necessarily represent direct violence, but foreground disorientating pacing and narrative that encourage audiences to anticipate violence at every turn in the narrative. Horeck and Kendall's collection combines essays on a range of European filmmakers, including Danish director Lars Von Triers (*Dogville*, 2003; *Antichrist*, 2009) and French directors such as Catherine Breillat, Gaspar Noé, and Bruno Dumont. Nikolaj Lübecker, in his contribution, cites Haneke's *Funny Games* as one of the most notorious instances of this manipulation. The combination of dark humour and nihilistic actions within *Funny Games* echoes Sluizer's approach to understated black comedy.

Spoorloos and Michael Haneke's Funny Games

Like *Spoorloos*, Haneke's *Funny Games* was initially promoted as a 'thriller' when it was released at the 1997 Cannes Film Festival. *Funny Games* opens on a French suburban family at their holiday home. This idyll is disrupted in the opening moments of the film when two nameless male intruders invade their home. The intruders begin coercing the family, including parents and young child, playing mind games that become physical assaults and ultimatums that are increasingly dangerous and indeed fatal for the family. This film brings an audience face to face with a gruelling type of relentless violence that engages with the ethical implications of on-screen violence.

As Catherine Wheatley observes, *Funny Games* uses satirical techniques which consciously play with audience awareness:

> cutting is moderately paced, speeding up at points of high tension; shot/reverse shots, point-of-view shots and lingering close-ups of various objects (a knife left on the boat, a set of golf clubs, the family dog, all of which will play an important role later in the narrative) function as generic signposts. (2009: 11)

Violence has a deliberate and conscious status within *Funny Games*. Disturbing violence is supposed to highlight how easily on-screen excess can be turned into a spectacle that desensitises an audience to violence's causes and effects. Haneke intends his films to be 'polemical statements against the American "barrel down" cinema' embodied by Hollywood blockbuster directors 'and its dis-empowerment of the spectator' (Wheatley, 2009).

This approach echoes Sluizer's focus and control in the filming of *Spoorloos*. It is clear from Dennis Alink's Dutch-language documentary *Sluizer Speaks* (2014) that Sluizer consistently prioritised his directorial vision for the project over commercial considerations of film production. While Sluizer claims credit for the film's distinct style and aesthetic, emphasising his directorial control over 'every single shot' of *Spoorloos*, he contends that this creative vision did not translate into financial reward: 'I decided on the camera positions. And whether to use a 75 mm or 50 mm lens. [But] my film may have been successful, but I haven't had my director's fee for *The Vanishing* yet. Zero. Zero dot Zero in 2013' (Alink, 2014).

Sluizer's *Spoorloos* and Haneke's *Funny Games* offer an unflinching exploration of human obsession and cruelty. Both films are based on a series of escalating psychological games. In *Funny Games*, the sadistic duo subject their victims to unspeakable physical and psychological torture throughout one night. In *Spoorloos*, upon coming face to face with the man responsible for Saskia's disappearance, Rex realises that he must voluntarily place himself in Raymond's psychological hold. As Raymond tells him: 'You can kill me. I acknowledge your right to do so. I'll take the risk. But you'll never know what happened to Saskia. I'm banking on your curiosity.'

Figure 7. Lemorne meets with Rex for the first time. (Credit to Anouk Sluizer)

In *Spoorloos*, as in Haneke's *Funny Games*, Sluizer's aim is not solely to shock his audience but to compel them to engage with the film's themes in more detail. Sluizer pushes viewers to think critically about why Rex subjugates himself to such a fate. The final scene pans the camera at an interior, low angle, panning across Rex entombed alive in the coffin. Sluizer, as a director, has a game to play: the cat-and-mouse pursuit between Rex and Lemorne echoes in the film's relationship with its audience.

This concluding scene is eerily faithful to Krabbé's story. In the novella, the realisation that plays out across Rex's face echoes the 'boundless panic' that 'rush[es] through his veins, faster than his blood' (2003: 111). Saskia is the final image within Rex's mind (as he gasps out her name as 'the walls [are] tight around him' with no hope). Rex's lighter – that he flashes desperately, repeatedly, as he scrabbles against the corners of the coffin – formed the closing shape of the golden egg. This evocative form has haunted Rex's dreams and, in turn, offered a premonition of his death. Rex's realisation that he has found his piece of forbidden knowledge, and the actual cost of that knowledge, paces throughout his mind: 'That this had been done to Saskia! That she had lain here like this, begging for him to come and save her, at the same time knowing there was no way he could possibly come…' (2003: 111).

In just over a minute, Sluizer extracts critical elements from the novella's closing pages and achieves several things. First, he is bringing the foreshadowing throughout the film to fruition. This final sequence recalls all the chief elements of the story. It emphasises recurrent imagery again and repeats earlier haunting strains of the film's music. A chilling sense of déjà vu overshadows the final sequence. Sluizer shows us the final moments of Rex's life, in which memory and the present blur into one until his mind eventually succumbs to death. Unusually, this is done without the splicing of flashbacks. Instead, the shot in the coffin fades out into the blurred shape of the golden egg, as the shape of the lighter forms the shape of the egg. A dying man is said to see his life pass before his eyes: Sluizer's *Spoorloos* is a reversal of this cliché since, in a sense, Rex has been frozen in time ever since Saskia's disappearance.

Spoorloos emerges as a darker manifestation of how art cinema and horror film can combine and depict more subtle types of horror. Some argue that Sluizer's film can feel oppressively cruel and nihilistic to its characters and audiences alike, undermining any notion of purging grief or catharsis that audiences may expect. In a mournful review published in 2022, for example, Ana Peres reflects on watching *Spoorloos* during the COVID-19 pandemic. Peres finds the film far too melancholy and claustrophobic compared to the more crowd-pleasing catharsis and enjoyment of the horror genre.

Peres remarks that, while watching *Spoorloos*, she sees an eerie parallel:

> emotions and lack of answers to their questions lead to a deep fear of their future as if something awful is waiting for them, making them unmotivated with no sense of control over their lives. Having an episode of existential dread is common, and taking into consideration the COVID-19 pandemic, it is expected that a lot of people have experienced this deep dread over the past couple of years. (Peres, 2022)

The existential dread that *Spoorloos* provokes is a classic feature of the post-horror film, denying audiences a traditionally satisfying resolution. By stretching out Rex's grief throughout the film, the audience sees grief's intricate, slowly unfolding impacts. So much so that audiences may feel complicit with willing Rex to discover the causes of Saskia's disappearance; this enhances the sense of psychological horror that permeates the film; the audience is forced to navigate voyeuristic fascination and sympathy.

Such effects, according to Church, are also not unusual within post-horror cinema. Post-horror frequently adopts attributes of 'modernist art films,' as a sub-category of film that he contrasts to classical Hollywood cinema. Modernist cinema 'frequently include[s] drifting, circular and open-ended narratives; ambiguous and psychologically complex characters; and various forms of spatial and temporal manipulation (including deliberate continuity violations, durational realism, and so on)' (Church, 2021: 8). However, there is a more sinister edge to Lemorne's behaviour which foreshadows how he will manipulate and deceive his victim. Lemorne's smoke-and-mirrors illusion of normality is acute during the scene when he meets Saskia. Throughout this scene, a ratcheting up of uncertainty inches Saskia and the audience closer to the seemingly inevitable and horrific conclusion. This effect is pertinent for discussing *Spoorloos* as a film that critics have described as 'nihilistic' and a play on 'existential dread' (Peres, 2022).

Social Tension and Awkwardness in *Spoorloos*

However, alongside this sense of existential dread, viewers can perceive other post-horror conventions within *Spoorloos*. A significant source of disquiet within post-horror cinema is watching protagonists attempt to navigate tense or awkward social situations in which they find it difficult to read social cues and etiquette. As protagonists become more involved in a situation or group, we realise that they cannot anticipate danger and that the social situation is more ominous than we might initially realise.

More recently, contemporary takes on this film have become prominent in European cinema. *Speak No Evil* (2022), directed by Danish director Christian Tafdrup, is one such instance. *Speak No Evil* focuses on a Danish couple, Bjorn and Louise, who are visiting their friends, whom they have only met once before, on holiday – a Dutch couple, Patrick and Karin. The story is of Bjorn and Louise's struggle to navigate an unfamiliar culture, with the domestic setting of Patrick and Karin's home gradually – and chillingly –

changing from a welcoming environment into an ominous comedy of errors as the host couple becomes more hostile through abrasive comments, aggressive behaviour, and disregard for dietary requirements.

The timid couple cannot seem to assert themselves as their hosts' attitude becomes more aggressive and violent. They are paralysed into going along with their hosts amidst their self-destructive desire to be polite. Before this point, the director crafts a series of tense, almost comically bizarre social encounters that are darkly humorous and frightening. David Gillota recognises this type of comedy in his study of comedy in American horror. Gillota writes that 'horror's awkward humor sheds light on anxieties about cultural differences or the disruption of social norms' (2023: 6). Quoting the theorist Stephen Prince, Gillota affirms the point that horror often 'dramatizes the tenuousness of the human world' – whether the 'breakdown of social rules and guidelines' of a collapse of the world in apocalyptic disaster or a pushing against the barriers of social acceptability (ibid.).

At the same time, there is an additional sense of dread beneath this awkward humour that discomforts the audience. Within *Speak No Evil*, the same audience that recognises the dark humour in social situations also perceives a genuine threat beneath the surface. This dread also arises within and overshadows *Spoorloos*. A similar focus on everyday discomfort and social acceptability is echoed in a later sequence in *Spoorloos* when we see how Saskia encountered Lemorne. Two critical moments of uncomfortable social awkwardness occur during the flashback to Saskia's abduction, narrated by Lemorne. The first follows a failed attempt by Lemorne to lure a woman into his car. He has inadvertently torpedoed his own plot by sneezing into a handkerchief drugged with chloroform.

Recovering from the incident, Lemorne emerges from the gas-station restroom with a knowing smirk on his face. The camera depicts a refracted view of Lemorne looking into the mirror as he straightens himself out before returning to the station. The sounds of the memory enhance the mundanity of the setting – the murmur of the crowd, the echo of the cashier's conversation, and the coffee machine. This brief sequence is surprisingly sinister despite Lemorne's haphazard approach. Lemorne's laughter shows that hindrances to his plan are amusing distractions rather than major obstacles.

An increased focus on the ordinary features of the settings also characterises the mise-en-scène in the lead-up to Saskia's abduction. There is minimal attentiveness to immediate danger and tension. This is equally apparent in the subsequent shot, which takes place in front of the coffee machine. Lemorne seems to have given up on his task for the day and is buying a coffee before leaving the station. The long-shot angle shows Saskia casually strolling to the machine and searching her purse for change. She realises that she does not have the change needed for the machine. Lemorne is the nearest customer to ask for help. She asks Lemorne for the change in her faltering French, and their first – and only – exchange begins.

The editing of the scene emphasises that Saskia has only encountered Lemorne by random chance. It begins with Lemorne's near-miss with another potential victim at the gas station. This unnamed customer agrees to help Lemorne, seemingly incapacitated by his false arm cast, to connect a trailer to the back of his car. With the anonymous female customer willing to get into the passenger seat, Lemorne prepares chloroform. As he is about to administer the drug, he is caught off guard and sneezes into the chloroform. Forced to retreat from his potential victim, Lemorne enters the communal bathroom. He leaves the puzzled woman to walk back alone, unaware of the fate that she has been spared. Only after Lemorne has given up on the abduction does Saskia come into the station to buy drinks.

Here, for the first time and, ironically, in the film's closing sequences, the film brings the two main characters together. Rather than focusing on Saskia's point of view, we see her through Raymond's eyes – open, enthusiastic, and vulnerable. The film's non-chronological structure takes the audience, step by step, back to the original crime scene. This structure is more like a procedural crime drama than a horror film. Mark Kermode describes the particular affect that such an awkward situation evokes. He writes:

> The original version of the *Spoorloos* […] is about a couple traversing a border, into a country where one of them is trying to speak the language. Part of what's going on is about language barriers and […] it's about the ways in which not understanding language can create tensions and where you are confronted with situations where you can't figure out whether situations are wrong. (Kermode and Mayo, 2022)

Saskia's vulnerability here is heightened by the language barrier between her and Lemorne. This barrier allows Lemorne, in character with a killer who moves under the radar, to more easily manipulate and distort her perceptions. Saskia is enthusiastic about her rudimentary French and about opportunities to practise during her holiday. However, when Lemorne complements her French, she jokingly calls him a 'liar.' The language barrier removes any caution Saskia may have around a stranger. Lemorne now has a legitimate reason to talk to her. He does not need to sneak into her trust under false pretences now. This approach contrasts with the nervous and fumbling manner he adopts in other abduction attempts.

When Saskia spots the keyring that Lemorne has on his car keys, she is delighted by its appearance. She manages to bring the words together in French to describe her enthusiasm. As she stammers out her words, the focus on trying to communicate limits her capacity to pick up on Lemorne's body language and cues: 'Because I love him [Rex] very much [...] and [he] also has a name with Rex, Roel, Roger.' By the end of their meeting, Saskia is enthusiastic to join Lemorne at his car. He does not need to remove her forcibly. As they stand talking near the drinks machine, she spies Lemorne's car keys in his hand. Delighted by the gold 'R' shape, she says she would like to buy one as a surprise gift for Rex.

The camera rests in close-up on Lemorne's face as he clocks this opportunity. His self-possession is evident from small movements – the slow closing of his eyes and his calm nod. Lemorne masks his efforts to lure Saskia to his car with convincing detail. He is a salesman with boxes of the keyrings in his car. Saskia only has to step outside with him into the car park to find the keyring she wants for Rex. The following shots unfold in a blur. Saskia steps out of the station with Lemorne. She catches her last glimpse of Rex in the far forecourt. When she arrives at Lemorne's car, he points at a box in the back that he claims contains the keyring. Saskia is not wary or suspicious and is at her most vulnerable.

Saskia has one final moment to save herself when Lemorne invites her to sit in the car's passenger seat under the guise of showing her the box's contents. She hesitates, understanding, on a subconscious level, that something is suspicious about Lemorne's invitation. Like the protagonists in *Speak No Evil*, she is placed in a socially difficult and awkward situation where she feels she cannot say no. She is trapped by the fear of undermining her social acceptability. She then catches sight of a photo on the dashboard with Lemorne and his daughters. Reassured by his family-man image, she gets into the car. The quest to save Saskia starts from this moment since this is the moment at which her fate is sealed. The moment when Lemorne drugs her with the chloroform is an intense, prolonged sequence. This sequence shows Saskia's eyes widen in shock and struggle before the drug takes effect, and she slumps in the passenger seat. This shot is the pivotal moment in the film that brings home the brutal circumstances of Saskia's disappearance.

This focus on Saskia's terror may seem unusual. Throughout *Spoorloos*, Sluizer presents a series of sequences that are powerfully overshadowed by spectral images of Saskia as a presence who is no longer there. When she stands at the tunnel entrance, the music echoes in the background, and the blinding light at once illuminates her presence and makes her more translucent. *Spoorloos* recognises grief as an absence and registers within the film's mise-en-scène. Saskia is a now-absent presence that can no longer be seen, and this absence echoes throughout the film. It is this type of affect that Richard Armstrong recognises as being found within the formal qualities of film. Saskia is the type of girl who is 'no less "present" for her very absence' (2012: 40). Despite her ghostly and ephemeral presence, she seems 'increasingly vivid.'

Figure 8. Saskia and Rex are together for the final time. (Credit to Anouk Sluizer)

This type of effect is a 'product of such moments of precipitate presence […] simultaneously calling into question the veracity of what we see, while making it apparent that "something" is present' (ibid.). Despite having under ten minutes of screen time, Saskia is a vivid presence whose memory and image haunt the entire film. Ter Steege's performance has something to do with this. She gives Saskia a liveliness that conveys an individual at a unique point in youth and on the cusp of the prime of life. As Geoffrey McNab writes, 'You probably haven't heard of Johanna ter Steege, even if the legendary American film-maker Stanley Kubrick once called her the best actress he knew' (2009). This vivid imagery is, at the same time, a reflection of the cyclical or circular narrative within *Spoorloos*, with the figure of Saskia echoing reverberations of traumatic loss.

Trauma and Flashback in *Spoorloos*

The structure of *Spoorloos*, with its strategic use of flashbacks and recurrent dreams, is a deliberate artistic choice that effectively conveys the psychological trauma experienced by the characters. These cinematic techniques, commonly associated with psychic trauma, have been a consistent pattern in cinema since its early days as a form of entertainment, as noted in Church's study of post-horror cinema.

> Indeed, cinema's visual grammar provided much of the vocabulary (such as flashbacks, screen memories, and so on) for Freud and other early elucidators of psychic trauma, while art cinema's formal innovations would later prove especially amenable to depicting trauma's distortions of memory/reality. (2021: 74)

While the term 'flashback' has been widely adopted in psychology, Maureen Turim retraces its history as a cinematic term, first and foremost, with origins in films including Alain Resnais's avant-garde *Hiroshima Mon Amour* (1957). As Turim writes, this 'flowering of an early cinematic modernism in the form of avant-garde movements' presented a more 'modernist inscription of the flashback, restoring some of the energy of dislocation and mimesis of thought and memory inherent in the flashback' (2013: 189). By the 1970s, psychologists were associating the experience of the traumatic flashback with Vietnam War veterans suffering PTSD. In turn, Vietnam War films of the 1960s absorbed this logic into their narrative structure. Such films depict flashbacks as 'mental events, portraying the memory of disturbed veterans' (ibid.).

Church refers to Nicolas Roeg's *Don't Look Now* (1973) as a telling example of how trauma and horror have reinforced each other on the cinema screen. '*Don't Look Now*'s disorienting use of graphic matches and intrusive images – though eventually revealed to be flashforwards instead of flashbacks – are a case in point' (ibid.). *Spoorloos*' use of similar imagery – also more in flashforward than flashback – is another case in point. The film effectively reflects individual trauma and grief as a discomforting presence with an aesthetic – through visuals, through audio – generating a feeling of slowness and distance. Sluizer effectively conveys the more out-of-body feelings and numbness of unfolding events via light. In this scene, where Saskia first strikes up a conversation with Raymond, the film is much more prosaic and minimalistic than Gothic. These locations include the busy forecourt, where Saskia disappears, and the crowd-filled station, where Saskia and Raymond first encounter each other. These scenes contrast the emotional darkness and raw human emotions in Rex's predicament.

The soundtrack is composed of synthesisers, punctuated by uncomfortably long moments of stillness – only to be interrupted by an almost subliminal, low-frequency throbbing that erupts into a loud crescendo. For instance, in the penultimate sequence, when Rex and Lemorne have returned to the gas station as the site of Saskia's original disappearance, the music throbs as Rex begins considering Lemorne's offer. It rises when he uncovers two sets of gold coins that he and Saskia buried and then tries to resist the seemingly inevitable outcome that he will drink Rex's drugged coffee. Aside from the closing scene (the closest scene to a jump scare within *Spoorloos*), each scene exemplifies the slower pace and disorientating visual framing. In light of *Spoorloos*' shocking twist ending, the film's use of recurring and symbolic motifs (often visualised via various objects resembling the shape of the golden egg) and the proleptic editing suggest the blurring of the past and present that the audience may have initially suspected to be Rex's grief-induced flashbacks about his lost girlfriend.

An early sequence in the gas station is an example of this effect. A combination of mobile camera shots and prolonged sequences takes us across all corners of the station. Our movement through these modern, transitional spaces is disorientating. It also evokes the disquieting sense of a journey beginning, almost as if it is a metaphor for Rex's position throughout the film. Rex has entered a hall of mirrors where he will be misled, toyed with, and given false hope.

The sequence sees an ordinary location become a place of horror and danger. *Spoorloos* exhibits many narrative features that Kevin Wynter and others identify with art-house cinema. The film prioritises realism over extreme violence. Instead, the film visually presents violence, emphasising how it may erupt out of random, everyday events. Sluizer is clear about his approach to pivotal scenes in *Spoorloos*, stating in a promotional interview that, 'in this film, I did my best to provoke, to magnify situations and characters in such a way that the audience would be disturbed' (Cordiay, 1989: 2). Sluizer certainly has a sly and practical understanding of how cinema can manipulate audiences.

Through the film's understated style, Sluizer draws attention to the calculating and meticulous characterisation of its villain, Lemorne. *Spoorloos* draws out the audience's curiosity about his intentions and malicious calculations. However, simultaneously, Sluizer depicts Rex's psychological unrest and turmoil after Saskia's disappearance. Through this depiction, *Spoorloos* adopts certain conventions now frequently associated with 'post-horror' cinema. These conventions include an open-ended, episodic narrative that moves between Rex and Lemorne and reflects the disorientating nature of grief. They also include a retreat from jump scares to emphasise more psychologically unpredictable characters instead. The film's alternate focus on Rex and Lemorne means that the audience is continually tossed back and forth between contrasting alternatives. Tarja Laine concludes, 'Even if we care about what happens to Rex, we are even more curious to find out what Lemorne's motives are, and this complexity renders the film into a moral exercise' (2011: 87).

David Church's description of 'post-horror' echoes the intensity of *Spoorloos*. In post-horror, 'familiar genre tropes become decentered via art cinema's formal expressiveness and narrative ambiguity, making space for characters and viewers alike to soak in contemplative or emotionally fraught moods, not to be shuffled along to the next abrupt scare' (2021: 12). Sluizer's film can be linking to a rapidly evolving cycle of art-house horror films that are still gaining recognition for their subversive use of similar conventions.

However, another aspect of *Spoorloos*' legacy should be addressed to provide a more complete picture of the film's influence. Any account of the film would be incomplete without a review of Sluizer's controversial Hollywood remake, which reversed each element and had the opposite reception to his original film. The following chapter will look at this remake more closely. We have explored the originality of the Dutch-language film and its underrated status as part of a still-growing trend of 'post-horror' cinema. It is now essential to analyse this remake since it also continues to be widely explored as part of *Spoorloos*' legacy. Interpreting a film that has been remade, particularly an American adaptation of a European success story, involves acknowledging a tension between the cultural context of the original and the new adaptation.

This remake, titled *The Vanishing* and released in 1993 in the US, was panned for reversing the original's climax. It was famously seen as an example of Hollywood's flawed appropriation of European cinema through expensive production values and simplified narratives, intended to make the films acceptable to global audiences. Actors with star power, Sandra Bullock and Kiefer Sunderland, were roped into the roles of the title couple (renamed from Saskia and Rex to Diane and Jeff), maintaining high publicity for the film. Jeff Bridges, also the star of the 1976 *King Kong* remake, was cast in Raymond's part shortly before filming commenced.

Negative reviews accompanied the release of this English-language remake. These reviews take issue with the complete reversal of the original twist ending. *The Vanishing* inserted a last-minute rescue for Jeff by his new girlfriend in the film's closing moments. The film, therefore, was accused of patronising American audiences for assuming they could not handle the dark twist of the original. Roger Ebert dismissed *The Vanishing* as a 'textbook exercise in the trashing of a nearly perfect film' and 'an American version, with an ending that is an insult to the intelligence and, by implication, to American audiences' (1993).

This book's final chapter will revisit this criticism of *The Vanishing* and address its legacy within the broader context of *Spoorloos*' reception and profile. This remake is an essential bookend to the story of *Spoorloos* and its production. Revisiting *The Vanishing* taps into debates about international horror cinema and the influence of different national cultures and industries. The following chapter argues that *The Vanishing* provides an insight into the influence of Hollywood on adaptations and remakes of European cinema at the turn of the millennium. *The Vanishing* is not a remake that should be forgotten due to its poorly comparing to Sluizer's original film. Instead, it is a necessary part of understanding *Spoorloos* and its status as an influential work of European cinema.

Chapter 6: Adaptations and Transformations

Sluizer's own Twentieth Century Fox remake of his original film, *The Vanishing* (1993), features a star cast, but was panned for reversing the original's climax and seen as an example of Hollywood's flawed appropriation of international cinematic traditions. The film features drastic departures from the original. Saskia and Rex are renamed Diane and Jeff (played by Sandra Bullock and Kiefer Sunderland, respectively). Raymond becomes Barney (with a stiff performance from Jeff Bridges). *The Vanishing* is an example of what Iain Robert Smith calls a 'transnational adaptation' in world cinema. This term refers to Hollywood remakes of original European films, transforming them through expensive production values and simplified narratives to make them acceptable to global audiences. This type of adaptation is especially grating since 'world cinema has often been defined explicitly in opposition to Hollywood, with various national cinemas held up as offering alternatives to the dominant American paradigm' (Smith, 2017: 4). This part of *The Vanishing*'s legacy highlights the need for a nuanced understanding of the contexts in which audiences view horror films.

Revisiting *The Vanishing* remake taps into timely debates about how international audiences see horror and how different national industries influence audience responses to horror cinema. Jeff Bridges, a star of the 1976 *King Kong* remake, was cast in the part of Lemorne shortly before filming commenced. Sluizer made significant changes to the original film in his remake, replacing the European location with US locations, including Washington State. Shot in the classical Hollywood style, this shift is a significant departure from the original and alters the tone and impact of the narrative. Sluizer supplements a memorable twist with a happy ending, where Jeff is rescued from the twisted fate that Barney (Lemorne's equivalent) inflicted on him. Both popular and scholarly writings have dismissed the film, agreeing that compared with the original, the remake seems like 'sacrilege – a vulgarization of a film that already seemed perfect' (Ebert, 1993).

The consensus is that this is a lacklustre attempt to reconcile a noirish-style thriller with Hollywood narrative conventions. Indeed, *The Vanishing*'s structure follows Hollywood conventions, including predictable narrative pacing, average shot durations, and jump scares enhanced by the diegetic need for suspense followed by cathartic resolution. However, the corny aesthetics throw Sluizer's original aesthetic minimalism in *Spoorloos* into sharp relief. The status and profile of *Spoorloos* – as an unexpected commercial success and, indeed, a visually unusual and distinctive film – heightened such derision. *The Vanishing* gives only scant attention to Barney's psychology while following the same noticeable and obvious plot lines of the original film.

In Sluizer's remake, Lemorne (now renamed Barney) undergoes a significant transformation. He is no longer an urbane and trustworthy family man, but instead, Bridges' rather stiff performance makes him more unreadable than intriguing. Too little of the film focuses on his backstory and the perverse justification for his experiment. Instead, his plot is secondary to the emerging love story between Jeff and his new girlfriend, Rita. In the original film, the new girlfriend, Lieneke, is reluctant to encourage Rex to uncover what happened to Saskia.

The postcards from Lemorne only provoke suspicion ('he's playing with you. He's followed the story through the papers and wants to see how far you'll go'). In *The Vanishing*, Rita (played by Nancy Travis) undergoes a significant transformation, becoming an amateur sleuth alongside Jeff. This change in her character alters the dynamic of the story, especially when she discovers Jeff's mawkish, obsessive diary entries that detail his continuing love for Diane ('Swear to God, Diane. I search for you everywhere. In passing cars. Over Rita's shoulder when we embrace. I cannot stop'). *The Vanishing* is about Jeff and Rita's dogged pursuit of truth rather than a melancholy meditation on the painful nature of loss. Rita is the one who eventually deduces the identity of the suspect and can rescue Jeff just before he is entombed in the ground.

By transforming this ending, Sluizer overturns his original film's more morbid and memorable themes. The appeal of the original emerged from how it depicted Rex's obsession and intrigued the audience's curiosity about the motives behind Lemorne's dangerous desire to test his own capacity for evil. Like many psychological horror films, *Spoorloos* deliberately takes its time to create suspense, slowly making its characters second guess themselves and, eventually, building suspense until a final scene that will keep audiences thinking about the film even weeks after watching the closing credits.

By contrast, *The Vanishing* relies upon a conventional cause-and-effect structure and departs from the realist aesthetics and narrative structures deployed in *Spoorloos*. Rita's action, rather than Jeff's psychology, is the main driving force in *The Vanishing*.

In contrast to the understated screenplay of the original, the remake is peppered with bombastic dialogue that undermines the slowly evolving dynamic between the three central characters. The first letter from Barney, promising to share information about Diane, is met with brazen confidence from Jeff rather than tormented fear: 'This letter's the first break I've had. I can nail this fucker!'

This dialogue belongs to a B-movie or police procedural drama. Considering that the remake flopped with US critics and audiences alike, for what appear to be at least some of the same reasons, should one conclude that Sluizer made a mistake in re-directing his own film for a more Hollywood market? I would say no, since even the more disparaging reviews acknowledged the filmmaking prowess, which was praised even while the overall film was derided. Malcolm Johnson writes, 'Until its over-the-top climax, which combines absurdity with one flash of slasher stuff, the American remake proves an intriguing variation on the first film' (2018). The climax in the remake significantly alters the tone and impact of the film, departing from the more subtle and psychological elements of the original.

The contrast between the original and the remake also serves to underscore the psychological elements in *Spoorloos*. Understanding the genre is crucial to grasping the characters and their relationships within *Spoorloos* and *The Vanishing*. The type of film we perceive *Spoorloos* to be hinges on our interpretation of the characters and their relationships. *Spoorloos* is a hybrid film that melds elements of horror and psychological thrillers. In *Spoorloos*, all that is familiar is rendered unfamiliar or 'uncanny' (unheimlich) by the experience of grief, and Rex can no longer anchor himself in the present. This psychological element adds a layer of intrigue for the audience.

As Freud famously states, 'the uncanny' is the unnerving provocation that is so frightening due to it recalling a memory of a repressed affect or emotion. 'It may be true that the uncanny [unheimlich] is something which is secretly familiar [heimlich-heimisch], which has undergone repression and then returned from it, and that everything that is uncanny fulfils this condition' (2003: 245). In terms of these uncanny archetypes, Lemorne is a perverse reflection of Rex's character and emotion, displaying an obsession with a form of forbidden knowledge that is a dark reflection of the obsession that Rex displays in his search for Saskia.

Lemorne is almost animalistic elsewhere – he observes and sets a trap for his prey, Rex. Rex is most explicitly animalistic when he cannot resist his impulse to follow Lemorne to France to take up the offer to discover what happened to Saskia. Returning to Freud and his idea of the uncanny, the uncanny is strange and eerily familiar. It is also associated with double characters or 'doppelgängers.' These doppelgängers are often telepathically linked through a psychic connection, which allows doubles to understand each other and anticipate what the other might do. According to Gry Faurholt, the doppelgänger appears in two forms: it is either 'the alter ego or identical double of a protagonist who seems to be either a victim of an identity theft perpetrated by a mimicking supernatural presence' or 'the split personality or dark half of the protagonist, an unleashed monster that acts as a physical manifestation' of the dark side of the subject (2009).

We have already seen that the metaphor of the golden egg plays a central part in *Spoorloos*, reflecting the emptiness and loneliness of Saskia and, eventually, Rex's fate. The metaphor of the doppelgänger has equal resonance for *Spoorloos*, providing a credible framework for interpreting the relationship between Lemorne and Rex. The two are an apt pairing: Lemorne is a man with a calculating investment in exploring the extremity of his own actions (a perverse ambition with roots in his sociopathic personality), while Rex is a victim whose actions are framed by an equally intense focus on knowledge and truth at all costs. Rex's name has a strange symbolism: it is a name for a king and a familiar name for a dog, suggesting he is both heroic and vulnerable – a transitional rather than a one-dimensional character.

By contrast, *The Vanishing* retreats from these nuances and ambiguities. In *The Vanishing*, the arguments between Jeff and Rita, as a new couple, become a dominant part of the plot, with emotions between them dictating the film's structure. The heavy-handed dialogue becomes mawkish at various points throughout *The Vanishing*'s screenplay. This snippet of Rita's dialogue with Jeff could be from a mid-1990s romantic comedy: 'If you ever want to move on with your life, if you want to be just alive again, then this is your last chance. I love you but you must decide to be with me, or I'm gone. Let her go, Jeff.' By contrast, the dialogue in *Spoorloos* is more enigmatic, adding to the mystery and suspense of the film.

The chess game between Rex and Lemorne, with Lemorne as the dark, calculating game master – becomes redundant. *Spoorloos*, in contrast to *The Vanishing*, plays with language and language barriers. In the original, Rex and Lemorne engage in hostile wordplay, referring to the Tour de France that took place around the time of Saskia's abduction. Raymond's conversation is nearly insulting in its casual friendliness. He suggests that 'the way up to Ventoux is the best place to watch the Tour de France go by.' He shares dry comments about the Dutch cyclist Hendrik 'Joop' Zoltemek: 'Doesn't sound Dutch. Sounds more like a Mexican God.' Rex indulges in this wordplay, correcting Lemorne's pronunciation: 'it's Zoetemelk. Zoe-te-melk. It couldn't be more Dutch.'

The trivial nature of this conversation probes and taunts Rex's pain. Lemorne reminds Rex, again and again, of the worst aspect of this encounter with Saskia's abductor: that he knows his identity yet has no proof of his guilt, and the abductor has no urgency to reveal the truth to him. By contrast, being solely in English, *The Vanishing*'s script has no scope for this verbal play or distraction. Barney ploddingly relays his motives, emphasising his upper hand without any subtlety: 'That's why I don't need a gun. Your obsession is my weapon. It's like you are my laboratory rat. I provided the materials. You've built the cage.' All that is implicit in *Spoorloos*' screenplay becomes explicit and stripped of all eeriness and subtlety in *The Vanishing*.

The structure of *The Vanishing* also undermines the suspense within Sluizer's original film. There is little difference between Lemorne's plan and Barney's plot. However, *The Vanishing* opens, jarringly, with Barney's preparations: 'Excuse me, miss. Yes, I'm sorry to bother you. I'm looking for the post office. You are? Would you like me to give you a lift?' There is minimal build-up of suspense or anticipation. *Spoorloos*, by contrast, is more concerned with the malleability of the human psyche, with Lemorne projecting an image of respectability. In an early scene, after we have seen Rex deal with the loss of Saskia, Lemorne tests the acoustics of his rural holiday home to assess whether neighbours can hear noises and screams from his property. He conducts a series of tests with chloroform, complete with a pencilled notebook, to see how many minutes the drug will incapacitate a potential victim.

There is also a more sinister edge to Lemorne's behaviour which foreshadows how he will manipulate and deceive his victim. Lemorne's smoke-and-mirrors illusion of normality is acute during the scene in which he meets Saskia. Throughout this scene, a ratcheting up of uncertainty inches Saskia and the audience closer to the seemingly inevitable and horrific conclusion. *The Vanishing* stages these preparations far more awkwardly. Bridges lumbers into the shot, and when he mimes an act of suffocating a victim on his young daughter, the performance becomes more slapstick than sinister. As Tina Hassannia writes, Barney mimes the 'act of the suffocation framed in such a way that Bridges' hairy hands loom up close near the camera and start shaking in a kind of comedic pantomime. It's so effectively risible that the film kills right then and there any notion that Barney is actually dangerous or infallible' (2012).

The Vanishing has become a touchstone example of the argument that Hollywood or US remakes of international films are a form of cultural appropriation. William Uricchio offers a persuasive phrasing of this take, arguing that it 'seems as though Hollywood took a "local" Dutch product and reworked it into a "global" vernacular, a version easily acceptable to transnational audiences' (1999: 370). However, while *The Vanishing* is inseparable from *Spoorloos*' legacy, I am wary of drawing too direct or in-depth comparisons between the two versions. The controversy around *Spoorloos* and *The Vanishing* has led to long-standing tension between Hollywood and other international film industries.

In one sense, it is unusual that Sluizer was offered an opportunity to remake *Spoorloos* by Twentieth Century Fox. This remake was especially uncommon for a Dutch film. Cuelenaere, Joye, and Willems acknowledge that Hollywood is more closely connected to 'bigger film industries (e.g., France, the UK, Germany or Spain)' due to their larger economies, industry profile, and distribution connections. They recognise that 'smaller film industries (such as the Dutch and Belgian) are not only more dependent on governmental support but also deal with small markets' and, therefore, are more likely to be overlooked by Hollywood production companies (Cuelenaere, Joye, and Willems, 2019). Only the exceptional popularity of *Spoorloos* caught the eye of studio heads at Twentieth Century Fox and led to the invitation to Sluizer to direct the English-language remake.

The release of this English-language remake was accompanied by negative reviews that took issue with his complete reversal of the original twist ending. By inserting a last-minute rescue for Jeff by his new girlfriend into the film's closing moments, *The Vanishing* was accused of patronising American audiences for assuming they could not handle the original. *Time Out* witheringly described *The Vanishing* as a 'misjudged, compromised Hollywood remake of [Sluizer's] Dutch French thriller.' The magazine writes that 'Sluizer has held down his waywardly inspired child while studio and scriptwriter Todd Graff have lobotomised it with a sharp, cruel scalpel' (*Time Out*, 2012). According to his long-time collaborator Anne Sluizer, for Sluizer, the opportunity to direct *The Vanishing* remake by Twentieth Century Fox was a necessary career move and one he hesitated before accepting, since he expected to run counter to studio expectations (Sluizer, 2023). Stephen Jay Schneider adds further detail to this account, writing that

> Sluizer owned the rights to Krabbé's novel and was willing to sell them only if he could direct. Twentieth Century Fox thought highly enough of *Spoorloos* that they took Sluizer up on his offer, under the condition that Hollywood screenwriter Todd Graff be permitted to retool the script to make it more palatable for American audiences. (2002)

It seems evident that Twentieth Century Fox underestimated the chilling and unnerving appeal of the original *Spoorloos* and assumed that this approach would not appeal to US audiences. Many scholars have rigorously broadened this transatlantic debate to such a depth that it would be difficult to capture fully, or to do justice to, within this book. Melis Behlil recognises the deep-rooted nature of the 'love–hate' relationship between European film industries and Hollywood, writing that 'Hollywood's interest in remaking films from other countries has been a constant part of the business since the very early days of sound film.' However, films like *Spoorloos*, produced during the 1990s blockbuster phase in Hollywood with franchises including *Jurassic Park*, were released 'with the advent of "New Hollywood".' Behlil explains that the 'popularity of remakes in this [blockbuster] era is related to the studio's desire to use sources that are "presold" in other media, that have already proven their popularity in other markets' (2007: 94–5).

Echoing this question of cultural prejudice, the critical mistake of *The Vanishing* is sidelining the more horrific elements of *Spoorloos* in pursuit of producing a thriller with a twist ending in the Hitchcockian style. Yet this remake also highlights the originality of Sluizer's first film. *Spoorloos* may seem, with these traits, an exceedingly bleak film, yet its austere style points towards a pathos that powerfully generates lingering dread and wrestles with themes of loss and grief. In the love story between Rex and Saskia, *Spoorloos* offers glimpses of hope, with the force of romantic love able to reunify lovers after death; but whether or not these glimpses are merely examples of cruel or cynical playing with emotions is open to debate.

The Vanishing is a controversial part of *Spoorloos*' history. However, by acknowledging its place in Sluizer's filmography, we can gain a clearer understanding of the original appeal and popularity of the earlier film. Unlike its remake, *Spoorloos* can get under the skin of its viewers through psychological suspense or explicit violence. It is a film that can fit into many genres – horror, thriller, psychodrama – while approaching human emotions and grief through horror conventions that are still recognisable in contemporary cinema.

Afterword: *Spoorloos'* Legacy

Drawing together psychology, suspense, and pathology, *Spoorloos* offers up a villain and monster with desires and actions that are comprehensible within the 'serial killer' character type. It is also no surprise that *Spoorloos* leans towards the Gothic since the cinematic serial killer is also a kind of villain that brings the extreme and unpredictable world of the Gothic into the contemporary world. Brian Jarvis calls this 'serial killer shock value,' which he describes as existing within a 'profitable' market that 'both reflects and produces an apparently insatiable desire for images and stories of serial killing in a Gothic Hall of mirrors' (2007: 328). Horror is not in conflict with other genre conventions here, especially since both are mediated by the narrative structure of the Gothic, and especially the Female Gothic. The stylistic austerity and dark familial themes coalesce in *Spoorloos* in such a way as to solidly evidence the core themes of post-horror, thus representing how horror emerges from the cross-referencing between art and horror cinema. Praise of Sluizer's artistic vision in *Spoorloos* even went so far as to label him as a 'more intellectualised Hitchcock. Hitchcock in a beret' (Hinson, quoted in Schneider, 2002: 193). This artistic vision is something that should inspire and be appreciated by all who engage with the film. *Spoorloos*, unlike its remake, is able to get under the skin of its viewers, whether through psychological suspense or explicit violence.

Figure 9. Behind the Scenes of Spoorloos' *closing sequence. (Credit to Jan Wich)*

Spoorloos draws upon a longer and recognised tradition of art-house cinema to develop its slow-burn sense of dread and terror. The film's stylistic hybridisation of art and horror cinema has sowed seeds for ongoing generic growth and development in horror. *Spoorloos* has become a historically and generically significant film because of how it subverts expectations and cultures in horror cinema. Before *Spoorloos*' release, perceptions of evil and monstrosity were modelled by a first wave of 'slasher' franchises, featuring *Halloween*'s invincible Michael Myers (1979), *Friday the 13th*'s vengeful Jason Voorhees (1980), and *A Nightmare on Elm Street*'s sadistic Freddy Krueger (1984).

In contrast to these adrenaline-fuelled films, *Spoorloos* is more ambiguous, as is apparent from both prominent film critics' attempts to frame *Spoorloos* as a Hitchcock-style thriller and the grassroots efforts by Rotten Tomatoes and film-forum users calling it an underrecognised horror film. For these critics, the pathos-laden journey of the film's protagonist, Rex, traverses a narrative that seems so detached from the horror genre as to be scarcely considered part of it. In some ways, this is a familiar pattern for horror cinema since readers only have to look back to iconic films like *Psycho*, which received a mixed reception upon its release in 1960.

The sense of lingering dread *Spoorloos* so powerfully generates is symptomatic of a period that extends to other films and casts a stylistic and affective shadow of cinema. *Spoorloos* has a connection to the serial-killer film that grew in prominence during the period (it has been read, along with several other titles, as an example of the genre), drawing attention to the psychology and motives of this threat. Given the cultural familiarity of both the serial killer and the (often) female victim, it is worth reiterating how emergent this character type was in late 1980s films and media. *Spoorloos* may seem, with these traits, an exceedingly bleak film, yet its austere style points towards a pathos that powerfully generates lingering dread and wrestles with themes of loss and grief. In the love story between Rex and Saskia, *Spoorloos* offers glimpses of hope, with the force of romantic love able to reunify lovers after death; but whether these glimpses are merely examples of a cruel or cynical playing with emotions is open to debate.

Approaching a film like *Spoorloos* involves navigating a tension between, on the one hand, interpreting the possibilities of horror as an ambitious and unpredictable genre space that can renew itself again and again and, on the other, accounting for the tropes familiar to fans of the genre. As a film, it manifests a set of ambivalent tropes that provide some early foreshadowing of – if not direct inspiration for – later 'post-horror' films that would meditate on darker themes of loss and grief. As both critics and fans know, horror films can contain hidden depths about loss and mortality, both as works of entertainment and as artistically self-conscious works. *Spoorloos* is one contribution to this still-evolving tradition, and its unique approach to the horror genre is something that all fans and scholars should appreciate. Ultimately, across these chapters, this book brings different aspects of *Spoorloos* together to offer the first study of the film as a European horror film with a distinct and evolving legacy for modern-day cinema.

Bibliography

'The 100 Scariest Movie Moments No.55 "The Vanishing" *Spoorloos* 1988', *YouTube*, uploaded by SamkillGhost, 1 June 2011. Available at: www.youtube.com/watch?v=L7_2j-XPR_k&t=58s (Accessed 13 June 2023).

Aldam, R. (2022) 'Blu-rat Review – Henry: Portrait of a Serial Killer', *Backseat Mafia*. Available at: https://www.backseatmafia.com/blu-ray-review-henry-portrait-of-a-serial-killer/ (Accessed 15 December 2023).

Alink, D. (2014) *Sluizer Speaks*. Amsterdam: Molenweik Films.

Armstrong, R. (2012) *Mourning Films: A Critical Study of Loss and Grieving in Cinemas*. London: McFarland and Company Inc.

Augé, M. (1995) *Non-places: Introduction to an Anthropology of Supermodernity*. London: Verso.

'BFI Thriller on Tour' (2017) Independent Cinema Office. Available at: https://www.independentcinemaoffice.org.uk/tours/bfi-thriller-on-tour/ (Accessed 3 November 2023).

B.L. (2013) 'Beaune: il y a 31 ans, un accident de car faisait 53 morts sur l'autoroute A6', *France Info*. Available at: https://france3-regions.francetvinfo.fr/bourgogne-franche-comte/cote-d-or/beaune/beaune-il-y-31-ans-un-accident-de-car-faisait-53-morts-sur-l-autoroute-a6-294949.html (Accessed 27 December 2023).

Baran, S. (2023) 'Good Grief: Sorrow, Screams, and Silence in the Contemporary Horror Film', *Quarterly Review of Film and Video*. Available at: https://doi.org/10.1080/10509208.2023.2225402 (Accessed 27 December 2023).

Behlil, M. (2007) *Home Away from Home: Global Directors of New Hollywood*. Thesis: University of Amsterdam.

Billson, A. (2018) 'Stop the horror snobbery! I just want my jump scares back', *The Guardian*. Available at: https://www.theguardian.com/film/2018/nov/22/stop-the-horror-snobbery-i-want-my-jump-scares-back (Accessed 28 April 2023).

Bohn, S.A. (2014) 'If Not a Serial Killer, Then What Is Charles Manson?' *Psychology Today*. Available at: https://www.psychologytoday.com/intl/blog/wicked-deeds/201403/if-not-serial-killer-then-what-is-charles-manson (Accessed 15 December 2023).

Bondeson, J. (2002) *Buried Alive: The Terrifying History of Our Most Primal Fear*. W.W. Norton & Company.

Botting, F. (1996) *Gothic*. London: Routledge.

Brinkeme, E. (2014) *The Forms of the Affects*. Durham, NC: Duke University Press.

British Film Institute (1990) *Awards List: Spoorloos – The Vanishing – L'Homme Qui Voulait Savoir*.

Brook, D. (2020) 'The Vanishing (1988) – Studiocanal', *Blue Print Review*. Available at: https://blueprintreview.co.uk/2020/06/the-vanishing-1988-studiocanal/ (Accessed 18 November 2023).

Cagle, C. (2016) *Sociology on Film: Postwar Hollywood's Prestige Commodity*. New Jersey: Rutgers University Press.

Carroll, N. (1990) *The Philosophy of Horror, or, Paradoxes of the Heart*. London: Psychology Press.

Cavallaro, D. (2002) *Gothic Vision*. London: Continuum.

Cheded, F. (2018) 'The Subversive Horror of "The Vanishing"', *Film School Rejects*. Available at: filmschoolrejects.com/the-subversive-horror-of-the-vanishing (Accessed 17 November 2023).

Church, D. (2021) *Post-Horror Art, Genre, and Cultural Elevation*. Edinburgh: Edinburgh University Press.

Clark, N. (2019) 'Netflix's New Ted Bundy Biopic Has One Glaring Problem', *Vice*, 7 May. Available at: https://www.vice.com/en/article/mb8gmy/netflix-ted-bundy-biopic-zac-efron (Accessed 6 August 2024).

Clemens, V. (1999) *The Return of the Repressed: Gothic Horror from* The Castle of Otranto *to* Alien. New York: State University of New York Press.

Clover, C. (1992) *Men, Women, and Chainsaws: Gender in the Modern Horror Film*. Princeton: Princeton University Press.

Confrath, R. (1994) 'The Guys Who Shoot to Thrill: Serial Killers and the American Popular Unconscious', *Revue française d'études américaines*, no. 60, p. 143. Available at: https://www.jstor.org/journal/revufranetudamer.

Cordiay, H. (1989) 'An interview with George Sluizer', *Metro*, 81, pp. 1–12.

Coulthard, L. (2013) 'Interrogating the Obscene: Extremism and Michael Haneke', in *The New Extremism in Cinema: From France to Europe*. Edinburgh: Edinburgh University Press, pp. 180–91.

Cruz, R.L. (2012) 'Mutations and Metamorphoses: Body Horror Is Biological Horror', *Journal of Popular Film & Television*, 40(4), 160–8.

Cuelenaere, E., Joye, S., and Willems, G. (2019) 'Local flavors and regional markers: The Low Countries and their commercially driven and proximity-focused film remake practice', *Communications*. Available at: https://www.degruyter.com/document/doi/10.1515/commun-2019-2057/html (Accessed 12 August 2024).

D'Angelo, M. (2014) '*The Vanishing* is the original *Gone Girl*, with the truth learned at a price', *A.V. Club*. Available at: https://www.avclub.com/the-vanishing-is-the-original-gone-girl-with-the-truth-1798181863 (Accessed 22 December 2023).

De Semlyn, P., and Rothkopf, J. (2023) 'The best psychological thrillers to watch', *Time Out*. Available at: https://www.timeout.com/film/best-psychological-thrillers (Accessed 13 May 2023).

Derry, C. (1988) *The Suspense Thriller: Films in the Shadow of Alfred Hitchcock*. Jefferson, NC: McFarland.

Derry, C. (2009) *Dark Dreams 2.0: A Psychological History of the Modern Horror Film from the 1950s to the 21st Century*. Jefferson, NC: McFarland Books.

Dixon, W.W. (2010) *A History of Horror*. Rutgers University Press.

Doane, M. (1987) *The Desire to Desire: The Woman's Film of the 1940s*. Bloomington: Indiana University Press.

Donnelly, A.M. (2012) 'The New American Hero: Dexter, Serial Killer for the Masses', *Journal of Popular Culture*, 45(1), 15–26.

Drizou, M. (2016) '"Go Steady, Undine!": The Horror of Ambition in Edith Wharton's *The Custom of the Country*', in *Gothic Landscapes: Changing Eras, Changing Cultures, Changing Anxieties*, ed. Sharon Rose Yang and Kathleen Healey. London: Palgrave Macmillan, pp. 125–46.

Dyer, R. (2015) *Lethal Repetition: Serial Killing in European Cinema*. London: British Film Institute.

Ebert, R. (1991) 'The Vanishing Movie Review and Film Summary', *Roger Ebert*. Available at: www.rogerebert.com/reviews/the-vanishing-1991 (Accessed 18 August 2023).

Ebert, R. (1993) 'The Vanishing', *Roger Ebert*. Available at: https://www.rogerebert.com/reviews/the-vanishing-1993 (Accessed 28 January 2024).

Ebert, R. (2013) *Ebert's Bigger Little Movie Glossary: A Greatly Expanded and Much Improved Compendium of Movie Clichés, Stereotypes, Obligatory Scenes, Hackneyed Formulas, Shopworn Conventions and Outdated Archetypes*. Kansas City: Andrew McMeel Publishing.

Faurholt, G. (2009) 'Self as Other: The Doppelgänger', *Double Dialogues*. Available at: https://doubledialogues.com/article/self-as-other-the-doppelganger/ (Accessed 27 January 2024).

Foundas, S. (2014) '*The Vanishing*: The End of the Road', *The Criterion Collection*. Available at: www.criterion.com/current/posts/3340-the-vanishing-the-end-of-the-road (Accessed 6 August 2023).

French, P. (2009) 'Amsterdamned', *Guardian*. Available at: https://www.theguardian.com/film/2009/oct/25/amsterdamned-dvd-review-philip-french (Accessed 29 April 2024).

Freud, S. (2001 [1917]) 'Mourning and Melancholia', in *The Complete Psychological Works of Sigmund Freud*. London: Vintage, pp. 243–58.

Freud, S. (2003) *Beyond the Pleasure Principle and Other Writings*. London: Penguin.

Gillota, D. (2023) *Dead Funny: The Humor of American Horror*. New Jersey: Rutgers University Press.

Glasby, M. (2016) 'The Vanishing', *Total Film*, 6 May, pp. 102–7.

Goyaz, A. (2023) 'The Vanishing Has One of the Most Disturbing Endings Ever Made', *Movie Web*. Available at: https://movieweb.com/the-vanishing-disturbing-ending/ (Accessed 3 November 2023).

Greven, D. (2019) 'Review of *Robin Wood on the Horror Film: Collected Essays and Reviews*', *Cineaste*. Available at: https://www.cineaste.com/summer2019/robin-wood-on-horror-film-collected-essays-and-reviews (Accessed 20 November 2023).

Hassannia, T. (2012) 'Re-Make/Re-Model: The Vanishing (1988) vs. The Vanishing (1993)', *Spectrum Culture*. Available at: https://spectrumculture.com/2012/11/18/re-makere-model-the-vanishing-1988-vs-the-vanishing-1993/ (Accessed 27 January 2024).

Hawkins, J. (2000) *Cutting Edge: Art-Horror and the Horrific Avant-Garde*. Minnesota: University of Minnesota Press.

Hills, M. (2005) *The Pleasures of Horror*. London: Continuum.

Hodgkinson, S., Prins, H., and Stuart-Bennett, J. (2017) 'Monsters, madmen… and myths: A critical review of the serial killing literature', *Aggression and Violent Behaviour*, 34, 282–9.

Horeck, T., and Kendall, T. (2013) 'Introduction', in *The New Extremism in Cinema: From France to Europe*. Edinburgh: Edinburgh University Press, pp. 1–17.

Hutchings, P. (2004) *The Horror Film*. London: Pearson Longman.

'Interview – George Sluizer (THE VANISHING/SPOORLOOS)', *YouTube*, uploaded by Igor Leoni, 6 June 2020. Available at: www.youtube.com/watch?v=IZu0RseDGHI (Accessed 9 November 2023).

'Interview – Johanna ter Steege (THE VANISHING/SPOORLOOS)', *YouTube*, uploaded by Igor Leoni, 6 June 2020. Available at: www.youtube.com/watch?v=kDnT7JSMd3k&t=716s.

Jancovich, M. (1994) *American Horror From 1951 to the Present*. Keele: Keele University Press.

Jancovich, M. (2007) 'The Crack-Up: Psychological Realism, Generic Transformation and the Demise of the Paranoid Woman's Film', *Irish Journal of Gothic and Horror Studies*, 3 (8 November), 3–15.

Jarvis, B. (2007) 'Monsters Inc.: Serial Killers and Consumer Culture', *Crime, Media, Culture*, 3(3), 326–44.

Jenkins, P. (1994) *Using Murder: The Social Construction of Serial Homicide*. New Jersey: Transactions Press.

Johnson, B.D. (1993) 'The Vanishing', *Maclean's*, 106(7), 55.

Johnson, M. (2018) 'Review – The Vanishing (1993)', *Hartford Courant*. Available at: https://www.rottentomatoes.com/m/1042295-vanishing (Accessed 28 January 2024).

Joshi, S.T. (1999) *Great Weird Tales: 14 Stories by Lovecraft, Blackwood, Machen and Other*. Mineola: Dover Press.

Kawin, B. (2012) *Horror and the Horror Film*. London: Anthem Press.

Kermode, M. (1990) 'On George Sluizer', *Time Out*, 6 June 1990, p. 31.

Kermode, M., and Mayo, S. (2020) 'Top Ten: Films That Scared Mark Kermode', *Kermode and Mayo*. Available at: www.youtube.com/watch?v=Qdj_22hHRyM (Accessed 12 June 2023).

Kermode, M., and Mayo, S. (2022) 'Speak No Evil: Review by Mark Kermode', *Kermode and Mayo*. Available at: https://www.youtube.com/watch?v=pfK8dBey0Dsc (Accessed 15 December 2023).

Krabbé, T. (2003) *The Vanishing*. London: Bloomsbury Publishing.

Laine, T. (2011) *Feeling Cinema: Emotional Dynamics in Film Studies*. London: Bloomsbury.

Letha-Soman, N. (2020) 'Violence in Michael Haneke's Cinema, Explained', *The Cinemaholic*. Available at: https://thecinemaholic.com/violence-in-michael-haneke-cinema-explained/ (Accessed 8 January 2024).

Little White Lies (2022) '*Spoorloos* vs *The Vanishing*... Which Is Better?' Available at: https://www.youtube.com/watch?v=b2Tm9qcZKpM (Accessed 15 January 2024).

Lowenstein, A. (2022) 'Acting Your Age: Social and Psychological Horror in *The Amusement Park* and *Relic*', *Discourse*, 44. Available at: https://muse.jhu.edu/article/890362 (Accessed 8 January 2023).

Mallett, X. (2022) 'Glamorising serial killers like Jeffrey Dahmer through "true crime" shows has to stop', *Independent*. Available at: https://www.independent.co.uk/voices/serial-killers-jeffrey-dahmer-true-crime-ted-bundy-b2176716.html (Accessed 15 December 2023).

Mangham, A. (2010) 'Buried Alive: The Gothic Awakening of Taphephobia', *Journal of Literature and Science*, 3(1), 10–22.

Maslin, J. (1991) 'Review: How Evil Can One Person Be?' *New York Times*. Available at: https://www.nytimes.com/1991/01/25/movies/review-film-how-evil-can-one-person-be.html (Accessed 11 June 2023).

Mathijs, E. (2004) *The Cinema of the Low Countries*. London: Wallflower Press.

McDonald, K., and Johnson, W. (2021) *Contemporary Gothic and Horror Film*. London: Anthem press.

McGowan, T. (2011) *Out of Time: Desire in Atemporal Cinema*. Minneapolis: Minnesota University Press.

McNab, G. (2009) 'Kubrick's lost movie: Now we can see it…', *Independent*. Available at: https://www.independent.co.uk/arts-entertainment/films/features/kubrick-s-lost-movie-now-we-can-see-it-1516726.html (Accessed 10 January 2024).

Meares, J. (2021) 'The 29 Scariest Horror Movie Scenes of all Time', *Rotten Tomatoes*. Available at: https://editorial.rottentomatoes.com/article/scariest-horror-movie-scenes-of-all-time/ (Accessed 25 May 2023).

Meehan, P. (2011) *Horror Noir: Where Cinema's Dark Sisters Meet*. Jefferson, NC: McFarland.

Millar, B., and Lee, J. (2021) 'Horror Films and Grief', *Emotion Review*, 13(3), 171–82. Available at: https://doi.org/10.1177/17540739211022815 (Accessed 11 July 2024).

'The Most Terrifying Film? (The Vanishing, 1988)', *YouTube*, uploaded by Uncle Funtime, 4 April 2022. Available at: https://www.youtube.com/watch?v=Iccf7i-PIVQ&t=150s (Accessed 30 April 2024).

Murray, N. (2014) 'The Vanishing – Review', *Dissolve*. Available at: https://thedissolve.com/reviews/1174-the-vanishing/ (Accessed 30 May 2023).

Nayman, A. (2018) 'What's Streaming: The Original "The Vanishing" Still Terrifies, 30 Years Later', *Ringer*. Available at: https://www.theringer.com/movies/2018/9/5/17819076/the-vanishing-streaming-movie-influence (Accessed 29 May 2023).

Newman, K. (2001) 'The Vanishing', *The Criterion Collection*. Available at: https://www.criterion.com/current/posts/136-the-vanishing (Accessed 21 November 2023).

Nicholson, T. (2019) 'The 2010s Were the Decade When Horror Got Smart', *Esquire*. Available at: https://www.esquire.com/uk/culture/film/a30284121/elevated-horror-2010s-peele-eggers-aster-blumhouse/ (Accessed 21 April 2023).

Peres, A. (2022) 'The Vanishing: A Perfect Study in Existential Dread', *MovieWeb*. Available at: https://movieweb.com/the-vanishing-disturbing-movie/ (Accessed 8 January 2023).

Plan-Séquence (2022) 'DUTCH MASTERPIECES: The Vanishing – Spoorloos (1988)'. Available at: https://www.youtube.com/watch?v=yzi4GGtPkXM&t=213s (Accessed 18 January 2024).

Poe, E.A. (2007 [1843]) 'The Black Cat', in *Literature: Reading Fiction, Poetry, and Drama*, ed. Robert DiYanni. McGraw Hill, pp. 137–43.

Poe, E.A. (2015 [1844]) 'The Premature Burial', in *The Complete Tales of Edgar Allan Poe*. New York: Barnes and Noble, pp. 497–508.

Poe, E.A. (2022 [1845]) 'The Imp of the Perverse', *The Poe Museum*. Available at: https://poemuseum.org/the-imp-of-the-perverse/ (Accessed 14 July 2024).

Quandt, J. (2004) 'Flesh and Blood: Sex and Violence in Recent French Cinema', *Art Forum*. Available at: https://www.artforum.com/features/flesh-blood-sex-and-violence-in-recent-french-cinema-168041/ (Accessed 5 January 2024).

Rafter, N. (2006) *Shots in the Mirror: Crime Films and Society*. Oxford: Oxford University Press.

Roberts, L. (2014) 'The Violence of Non-Places', in *Tourism and Violence*, ed. Hazel Andrews. Farnham: Ashgate Publishing Press, pp. 13–32.

Rose, S. (2017) 'How post-horror movies are taking over cinema', *Guardian*. Available at: https://www.theguardian.com/film/2017/jul/06/post-horror-films-scary-movies-ghost-story-it-comes-at-night (Accessed 31 December 2023).

Rose, S. (2022) 'I called it "post-horror" – and now I've created a monster', *Guardian*. Available at: https://www.theguardian.com/film/2022/aug/02/i-created-a-monster-how-post-horror-it-comes-at-night-a-ghost-story (Accessed 19 July 2024).

Rosen, M. (1975 [1973]) *Popcorn Venus: Women, Movies and the American Dream*. London: Peter Owen.

Rubenstein, R. (1996) 'House Mothers and Haunted Daughters: Shirley Jackson and Female Gothic', *Tulsa Studies in Women's Literature*, 15(2), 309–31.

Rzepka, C. (2005) *Detective Fiction*. Cambridge: Polity Press.

Schneider, S.J. (2002) '*The Vanishing* and *Nightwatch*'. Available at: https://openjournals.uwaterloo.ca/index.php/kinema/article/download/996/1082?inline=1 (Accessed 28 January 2024).

Schneider, S. (2007) *100 European Horror Films*. London: Bloomsbury Publishing.

Schneider, S., and Sweeney, K. (2005) 'Genre Bending and Gender Bonding: Masculinity and Repression in Dutch "Thriller" Cinema', in *Horror International*, ed. Steven Jay Schneider and Tony Williams. Detroit: Wayne State University Press, pp. 180–201.

Seaton, M. (2003) 'Suffering Appeals to Me', *The Guardian*. Available at: https://www.theguardian.com/books/2003/oct/09/fiction (Accessed 7 November 2023).

Sedgwick, E. (2022) *The Coherence of Gothic Conventions*. London: Routledge.

Sheil, S. (2016) 'Death, Grief and Why Horror Films Truly Matter', *Talkhouse*. Available at: https://www.talkhouse.com/death-grief-value-horror-films/ (Accessed 11 July 2024).

Simpson, P. (2000) *Psycho Paths: Tracking the Serial Killer through Contemporary American Film and Fiction*. Carbondale, IL: Southern Illinois University Press.

Sluizer, A. (2023) Email to Christina Brennan, 23 April 2023.

Sluizer, G. (1988) *Spoorloos*. Argos Films.

Smith, I.R. (2017) *Hollywood Meme: Transnational Adaptations in World Cinema*. Edinburgh: Edinburgh University Press.

Spooner, C. (2007) *Contemporary Gothic*. London: Reaktion Books.

Time Out (2012) 'The Vanishing'. Available at: https://www.timeout.com/movies/the-vanishing (Accessed 3 March 2023).

Trussell, J. (2018) 'Prestige Horror Has Arrived', *Film School Rejects*. Available at: https://filmschoolrejects.com/prestige-horror-movies/ (Accessed 4 January 2024).

Tunney, T. (1990) 'Missing Presumed Dead Good', *Time Out*, 1033, p. 81.

Turim, M. (2013) *Flashbacks in Film: Memory and History*. London: Routledge.

Uricchio, W. (1999) 'Afterword: Rethinking the American Century', in *Media, Popular Culture, and the American Century*, ed. Kingsley Bolton and Jan Olsson. Bloomington: Indiana University Press, pp. 363–75.

Usborne, S. (2015) '10 best cycling books', *Independent*. Available at: https://www.independent.co.uk/extras/indybest/books/best-cycling-books-tour-de-france-chris-froome-national-bike-week-cyclist-10332192.html (Accessed 4 June 2023).

van der Waard, P. (2020) 'Gothic Themes in The Vanishing/Spoorloos (1988)', *Nick's Movie Insights*. Available at: https://www.nicksmovieinsights.com/2020/10/gothic-themes-in-vanishing-spoorloos.html (Accessed 2 June 2023).

Van Driel, H. (2004) 'Twee Vrouwen/Twice a Woman', in *The Cinema of the Low Countries*, ed. Ernest Mathjis. London: Wallflower Press, pp. 151–6.

Vanacker, S. (1995) '*Spoorloos/The Vanishing* 1988', *Dutch Crossing: Cinema of the Low Counties*, 19(1), 96–109.

Varndell, D. (2014) *Hollywood Remakes, Deleuze and the Grandfather Paradox*. London: Palgrave Macmillan.

Verstraten, P. (2016) *Humour and Irony in Dutch Post-War Fiction Film*. Amsterdam: Amsterdam University Press.

Wallace, D., and Smith, A. (2009) 'Introduction: Defining the Female Gothic', in *The Female Gothic: New Directions*. London: Palgrave Macmillan, pp. 1–12.

Walpole, H. (1982 [1764]) *The Castle of Otranto*, in *Three Gothic Novels*. London: Penguin, pp. 3–106.

Wells, J. (2020) '10 Most Disturbing Final Movie Scenes', *Screenrant*. Available at: https://screenrant.com/most-disturbing-final-movie-scenes/ (Accessed 6 January 2024).

Wells, P. (2000) *The Horror Genre: From Beelzebub to Blair Witch*. London: Wallflower Press.

'What the Critics Have Said about The Vanishing', Metro Press Pack, British Film Institute Reuben Library.

Wheatley, C. (2009) *Michael Haneke's Cinema: The Ethic of the Image*. Oxford: Berghahn Books.

Williams, L. (1999) 'Film Bodies: Gender, Genre, and Excess', in *Feminist Film Theory: A Reader*, ed. Sue Thornham. New York: New York University Press, pp. 267–81.

Wilmington, M. (1990) '"Vanishing" – a Thriller to Haunt You', *Los Angeles Times*. Available at: https://www.latimes.com/archives/la-xpm-1990-10-10-ca-1761-story.html (Accessed 28 November 2023).

Wood, R. (2018a) 'Disreputable Genre', in *Robin Wood on Horror Film: Collected Essays and Reviews*, ed. Barry Keith Grant. Detroit: Wayne State University Press, pp. 63–4.

Wood, R. (2018b) 'An Introduction to American Horror Film', in *Robin Wood on Horror Film: Collected Essays and Reviews*, ed. Barry Keith Grant. Detroit: Wayne State University Press, pp. 95–137.

Wood, R. (2018c) 'Psychoanalysis of Psycho', in *Robin Wood on Horror Film: Collected Essays and Reviews*, ed. Barry Keith Grant. Detroit: Wayne State University Press, pp. 19–28.

Wynter, K. (2017) 'An Introduction to the Continental Horror Film', in *Transnational Horror Cinema*, ed. Sophia Siddique and Raphael Raphael. London: Palgrave Macmillan, pp. 43–64.

Zinoman, J. (2018) 'Why Are We Ashamed to Call "Get Out" and "The Shape of Water" Horror Films?' *New York Times*. Available at: https://www.nytimes.com/2018/01/18/movies/get-out-the-shape-of-water-horror-oscars.html (Accessed 4 January 2023).